TED KENNEDY WATSON'S

GUIDE
TO
STYLISH
ENTERTAINING

TED KENNEDY WATSON'S

GUIDE
TO
STYLISH
ENTERTAINING

Written, styled & photographed by
TED KENNEDY WATSON

Foreword by Lisa Birnbach

GIBBS SMITH
TO ENRICH AND INSPIRE HUMANKIND

First Edition
22 23 24 25   5 4 3 2 1

Additional stock art by Shutterstock. Textures throughout: MaxyM, MM_photos, Nik Merkulov; v: Epine; 5 & 28: Anastasia Lembrik; 8: NatsukiYoshino; 22: Dario Lo Presti; 36: Yevheniia Lytvynovych; 51 & 70: vectortatu; 52: Bodor Tivadar; 53: Vlada Young; 63: AVA Bitter; 64: Sketch Master; 79 & 191: NataLima; 92: chempina; 104: Svesla Tasla; 108: MoreVector; 129 & 178: Channarong Pherngjanda; 134: mashakotcur; 156, 160 & 163: mamita; 186: Mashikomo

Published by
Gibbs Smith
P.O. Box 667
Layton, Utah 84041

1.800.835.4993 orders
www.gibbs-smith.com

Designed by Ryan Thomann
Printed and bound in China

Gibbs Smith books are printed on either recycled, 100% post-consumer waste, FSC-certified papers or on paper produced from sustainable PEFC-certified forest/controlled wood source. Learn more at www.pefc.org.

Library of Congress Control Number: 2021953389
ISBN: 978-1-4236-5729-3

TO MY MOM & DAD,
who taught me the importance of
breaking bread with those you
love, along with good manners
that stay with you a lifetime.
They loved a good party!

TO MY HUSBAND.
Over thirty years of hosting suppers and soirées and
it feels like we are just getting started. It has
always been "we," not "I," since day one, which has
made everything so much more meaningful and life oh so
sweet. We always know how to make it a party!

CONTENTS

Foreword by
Lisa Birnbach - IX

Introduction - 1

Let's Get
Started! - 6

To Dine - 22

To Party - 108

Flower Power - 148

To Sip - 166

To Taste - 176

Where to
Shop - 194

Sending My Love
& Thanks - 196

FOREWORD

By Lisa Birnbach

PEOPLE SOMETIMES MAKE THE MISTAKE of confusing graciousness with *fanciness* or *poshness*. (Trust me when I tell you neither of these words appear in my dictionary, yet you can find *bae*. Sigh.) The difference is enormous, and really lies at the heart of Ted's new book, *Ted Kennedy Watson's Guide to Stylish Entertaining*.

Fancy—an adjective that is now always accompanied by air quotes—is tolerable a few times a year, but is not a way to entertain that makes one's guests feel comfortable. Imagine being invited to Buckingham Palace and facing a place setting with flatware whose function you cannot even divine. You never know. It could happen, and it would feel like a test.

Graciousness replaces the focus from the host or hostess to the guests. How to make the experience more fun, more welcoming, warmer, and more pleasurable for all. That doesn't mean, for example, that one can only have five to dinner because you have exactly six matching place settings. Mix up what you have! Or, it could mean serving on paper or plastic; using (as I've learned from reading this book in manuscript) scarves as table runners, or scattering one's collection of dominoes, matchbooks, or tiny objets artfully around the table to provide some amusement for the diners.

Fussy is fraught. Easy is, well . . . easy. Have to serve the meal yourself? Leave great snacks in the living room while you plate supper. Can only find flowers at your neighborhood bodega? Put them in those cute Bonne Maman jars you have lying around, or other improbable vessels.

Now that everyone has food allergies, preferences, and specialized diets, life as a host has become complicated. You used to have a (usually) joyous moment of unveiling when dinner was served. Now there are fewer surprises, as catering must yield to the most allergic, save who is now not eating soy or Chilean sea bass. But that doesn't mean entertaining has to be clinical. Far from it.

I discovered my first delightful Watson Kennedy shop in 2010 while on a book tour in Seattle. I had to touch everything; the goods were so appealing! I met Ted and then his husband, Ted Sive, not long after, and have had the very good fortune of being entertained in two of their homes. I have witnessed close-up Ted's design, food, and sensualities. His houses smell fantastic, for starters.

A huge customer for fresh flowers (and failing that, large displays of fruit and vegetables), his rooms might be filled with lilies or paperwhites or tulips or lilacs. Then there are the soaps and scented candles in the bathrooms, the right music underscoring the visuals. The tables that are set with care. Lots of cheeses. Beautiful napkins. Great company. Their dog, Bailey, usually nestled by the table. It's comfortable and informal, but one leaves their houses feeling satisfied.

One has been ministered to. One's preferences and sensitivities have been considered. (And then I always leave with notes of what I want to buy next time I order from WatsonKennedy.com.)

Once I had the daunting task of hosting Ted for a meal at our apartment. He knew that I have a weakness for fried chicken and suggested we order that in (phew!) but brought a big bottle of Hendrick's gin, a small bottle of vermouth, and a bag of ice along to make martinis. Truly that made the evening elegant.

Take it from me—Ted Kennedy Watson is a dream host, and this book has a ton of ideas, large and small, to make entertaining at home creative and rewarding. It is a book you will return to again and again.

INTRODUCTION

———————

Entertaining has always been hugely important in my life, from very early on. My parents loved to entertain, and that tradition continues, since it holds very special meaning in our household. Sharing stories of some of the gatherings over the years brings back incredibly fond memories.

The basis of this book is to show you how to not let perfection hold you back from entertaining. It is the number one reason I hear from folks why they don't host guests in their home often. My goal is to show page after page of entertaining made fun, easy, and doable. Table settings, flowers, recipes, tips—an entertaining guide. My hope is that it becomes a go-to source for inspiration when you are planning your next dinner or party.

Starting to write a book about creative ways to be a host while we were quarantining was interesting, to say the least. We entertain lots! Not seeing and hosting friends and family has been one of the hardest parts. So maybe in that way, it was a perfect time to begin my book. It helped to remember how we reveled in and savored every moment with them all rather than letting those memories fade. Hosting a supper or cocktail party or guests for a long weekend rates pretty darn high on my happy meter. Breaking bread with those we care for is a huge expression of love.

When I was a little kid, I would fall asleep saying my prayers, asking God to help me play the perfect tennis match or get an A+ on a test. Fast-forward to being a grown-up and realizing perfection is not all that it is cracked up to be. Trying to make something perfect can be incredibly stressful and generally not tons of fun. I certainly tried to make many dinners and parties we were hosting perfect, but I realized I was having no fun at all. I would have a pit in my stomach through all of the preparations. That is when I became an advocate for imperfection, and when I did, I had a much better time at our parties and dinners, and I am sure our guests did too. As the years have passed, and I look back on all the swell gatherings we have hosted, the ones I remember most fondly are the ones I was most chill about. Now that is not to say they weren't a ton of work, but "perfection" was taken out of the equation. It freed me up to enjoy the small details along the way and not sweat the big stuff.

"What did you learn today?" It was a question my father posed to me at almost every supper with my parents. He thought it vital that you learn something new each day. So my hope is that you have many takeaways from these pages, whether you are a novice host or a seasoned pro. Please take some ideas, put your own spin on things, and make them your own. You have my blessing. Very few ideas are new; how you execute them is what makes them unique and interesting. Over the years, I have had the great fortune to learn from some pretty awesome folks. My guess is, many of them did not know I was watching so intently. To them I say, "Thank you!" Living creatively and being a stellar host takes thought and energy, but the benefits are worth it. So keep your eyes and ears open. Learn as you go. Learn something new every day.

THIS IS MY STORY. Better yet, it is our story. My husband and I have been entertaining together for over thirty years. The main thing I want to stress in these pages is that there is no one way to entertain. This is our way. This, again, is where I think people get nervous and start to compare, and that creates anxiety, so they don't entertain. That truly makes my heart ache. We have derived so much pleasure over the years from entertaining, in both big and small ways. I want you to experience that pleasure. Much like how you dress or style your home, how you entertain should be all about you. You are the host. If you have an incredible time, most likely so will your guests.

This book is a love letter to entertaining and all the family and friends who we have been so fortunate to celebrate with over the years. I hope it speaks to you and ignites a passion for inviting folks over for a drink, a meal, or a party and all the good times those bring and memories they create.

"Creativity takes courage."
—Henri Matisse

Host, noun:
someone who
entertains guests
or strangers in
"their" home.

"MY MISSION IN LIFE IS NOT MERELY TO SURVIVE BUT TO THRIVE & TO DO SO WITH SOME PASSION, SOME COMPASSION, SOME HUMOR AND SOME STYLE."

—MAYA ANGELOU

LET'S GET STARTED!

WHY ENTERTAIN?

For me, the number one reason to entertain has centered smack dab on wanting to show love to those closest to me and spend quality time with them in an environment we have created. To have them in our home and treat them with the utmost of care for the time they are there, to make them feel special, is my reason, but you certainly may have another. There is no wrong answer. My main thought is that entertaining should stem from something that results in joy for both the host and the guests. If a sense of joy is missing, believe me, the guests will feel it. Bottom line: only host a gathering

if you really want to do it. Often, I think people entertain out of a sense of obligation, which can sometimes be just fine, but other times can sap all the enjoyment out of getting folks together for fun. The best hosting is when you are truly having a good time at your own gathering. Guests can feel the energy a host emanates. There is usually quite a bit of work involved, even for a small fête. Asking others to help or co-host can also bring an element of delight and lighten the work load. Ultimately, you want to have a terrific time at your own gathering!

Gather, verb:
to bring together.

 ## things that
MAKE YOUR HOME AND EVENT
MAGICAL WHEN HOSTING

FLOATING CANDLES LIT IN YOUR
FILLED BATHTUB IS DREAMY.

PLACE VOTIVE CANDLES ON WINDOW
LEDGES FOR A LOVELY GLOW AND
LITTLE BITS OF UNEXPECTED DRAMA.

HAVE LITTLE BLOOMS EVERY-
WHERE: ON SIDE TABLES, AT THE
BAR, IN THE BATHROOM, ETC.

SET LITTLE BOWLS OF NIBBLES,
LIKE GOLDFISH CRACKERS OR
CASHEWS, HERE AND THERE.

HAVE DISPOSABLE CAMERAS AT THE
READY AND ENCOURAGE GUESTS TO
CLICK THROUGHOUT THE EVE. IT'S
OLD SCHOOL, BUT IT IS SUCH A TREAT
TO SEE THE PHOTOS LATER AND
HAVE KEEPSAKES OF THE EVENT.

MAIL SAID PHOTOS IN NOTES
TO GUESTS FOR A SWEET
REMINDER OF YOUR PARTY.
THEY MAKE GREAT BOOKMARKS!

SET OUT CORKS FROM BOTTLES
OPENED THAT EVE FOR THE TAKING.
SWEET MEMENTOS OF YOUR SOIRÉE.

FILL A BOWL BY THE DOOR FOR
GUESTS TO TAKE SOMETHING
WHEN THEY DEPART—BOTTLES
OF SPARKING WATER, ORANGES,
LITTLE BOXES OF CARAMELS,
AND PACKETS OF ASPIRIN.

SEND TEXTS TO YOUR GUESTS
THE NEXT MORNING THANKING
THEM FOR ATTENDING.

PUTTING TOGETHER
A GUEST LIST

Be it a small gathering or a large fête, who you invite can make all the difference in the success of a dinner or party. **THE MIX IS KEY.** With the goal of all your guests having a swell time, mixing up the guest list points you in that direction. You are the director in this production. Seat the banker next to the artist. The dancer next to lawyer. The mom who homeschools her kids next to the writer. Same goes for a party invite list. Mix it up. Variety is what makes the world the fabulous place that it is. From the recent college grad to the retired dentist, the success of a gathering ultimately comes down to your guests and how much enjoyment they are generating and having. Some like to seat couples apart and others like them close by or side by side or across from one another. Again, no wrong answer. We like to mix things up and have couples apart to begin the meal. For the dessert course, we have folks change seats, which livens things up. For a party, we move about introducing folks as the gathering begins.

WE LOVE TO SEND A MORE FORMAL PAPER INVITATION in the mail, as it is so uncommon these days and therefore more special. This requires more advance work. Get creative. We printed an invite and folded it in a diaper for a festive baby shower we hosted for the closest of friends. People still talk about the invite and party years later.

ALWAYS ASK FOR PEOPLE TO RSVP. It helps you tremendously when figuring out how much food and drink to purchase, and it helps with your seating chart. Biggest thing, it is just good manners for guests to let you know if they can or cannot attend.

RSVP: to respond to an invitation

THE ART OF ENTERTAINING

I LIKE TO THINK OF ENTERTAINING AS AN ART FORM and that we are all artists. Give each one of us a canvas, and we will all paint something different. But equip us with a little training and our canvases will look more refined and we will be much more confident as we tackle the task. My hope is this book is either a starting point, if you are new to hosting, or a brush-up course, if you already excel at hosting, giving you ideas to add to your entertaining arsenal. Then it is up to you to put your own spin on things to make them your own, be you a novice or a pro.

Happiness is not having what you want. It is appreciating what you have.

{Sometimes, the accidents that happen along the way can be beautiful too.}

FEELING LOVED

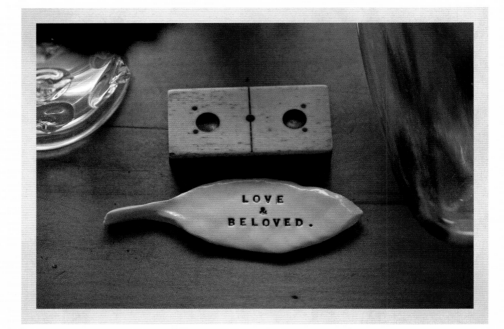

Making your guests feel comfortable and loved is, to me, what being a good host is all about. The minute they arrive in your home, you want them to feel cared for. Details like a little vase of beautiful blooms on a side table get noticed. The scent of the Diptyque candle fills the air, adding another layer of comfort. Music becomes part of the experience. A drink is offered within minutes and the weight of the world starts to melt away. "Care for your guests as you would like to be cared for" is my mantra. They are in your hands at the moment, feeling taken care of, feeling loved.

MAKE A LIST,

MAKE LISTS. Lists keep you organized. Lists can calm you when things go awry.

CREATIVITY IS KEY. Whether you are new to entertaining or a seasoned pro, it is what guests will remember long after the supper or party.

BE RESOURCEFUL. Just because you can spend lots of money on a gathering does not mean you have to do so. Use what you already have.

THE SMALL DETAILS MATTER. They are usually the most memorable part of a party. Make them count.

ENJOY YOUR OWN SOIRÉE! How much fun you are having at your own gathering is often an indication of how much fun others are having. Relax.

MAKE A LITTLE, BUY A LITTLE. Take the advice of my beloved Ina Garten. Your guests are not going to have a better time if you cook everything from scratch. This tip will save your sanity time and again.

ASK FOR HELP ALONG THE WAY. Enlist friends and family to help. If they're not available, think about hiring someone to lend a hand. But absolutely ask for help if you need to.

GET AS MUCH DONE AS POSSIBLE BEFORE FOLKS ARRIVE. This is key. Your enjoyment depends on it. Plus, no one wants to watch you peel carrots when you should be chatting with your guests.

THE POWER OF HIGH/LOW. Not everything needs to be top shelf. If you are serving lobster, which ate up much of your budget, think of using flowers from your yard so you don't need to spend money on flowers. High/low to me makes dinners and parties much more layered and interesting.

CHECK IT TWICE

YOUR HOME AND YOUR TABLE ARE YOUR CANVAS. Create your gathering the very best you possibly can, then stand back and admire your work. Any tweaks can be made for your next dinner or party. But for the one at hand, take satisfaction in knowing you did your best.

WHY HOST A DINNER OR PARTY?

Being clear on why you want to host a gathering is super important from the start. Is this for pure enjoyment? Is it out of obligation? Nailing down your expectations of the event ahead of time will enable you to be present in the moment, which will lead to you having a better time. Hosting a gathering for your husband's boss is quite different from an event filled with your best pals. Both can be thoroughly enjoyable, but the expectations will be different.

"Think of giving not as a duty but as a privilege."
—John D. Rockefeller, Jr.

WHAT MAKES A GREAT HOST?

Hands down, the number one thing for so many folks I talked with about this is that **THE HOST IS RELAXED.** Nothing takes a gathering down quicker than the host being a stressed-out mess. A good host—no, make that a great host—enjoys their own party! It really is such a simple concept, but it is not so easy in practice. Preparation is the key that helps a host chill once that first guest arrives. Having prepared as much as possible in advance means you won't be worrying about a million little details once people arrive. You want to be out and about with your peeps having fun. Sure, you had a mental checklist rolling around your brain while you are laughing at that funny story your friend just delivered, but you were present. You were in the moment. If enlisting the help of a few friends once they arrive can calm your nerves, do it. Most people are happy to lend a hand, and it makes them

feel included. The more you have done before you open the door for the first guest, the more relaxed you will be. If you remember anything from this book, remember that you don't have to be perfect to be an awesome host. It is often the little flaws that make for a great story or a cherished memory. **PERFECTION RARELY PUTS GUESTS AT EASE.** A spilled drink or dropped appetizer can actually get the party started. People relax a little. It is life. A really good life where you are the host!

what to do
BEFORE GUESTS ARRIVE

TURN ON YOUR
FAVORITE MUSIC.

POUR YOUR FAVORITE
LIBATION IN YOUR
FAVORITE GLASS.

GO TO YOUR CLOSET
AND PULL WHAT YOU
WOULD LIKE TO WEAR.

SIP SAID BEVERAGE.

TAKE AN EXTRA-LONG
SHOWER OR BATH, ALL THE
WHILE THINKING OF THE
FUN EVE AHEAD AND HOW
FORTUNATE YOU ARE.

SIP AGAIN.

GET DRESSED, BEING
SURE TO ADD ONE PIECE OF
CLOTHING OR JEWELRY
YOU ADORE.

SIT FOR A FEW MINUTES AND
ENJOY THE REST OF YOUR
DRINK. AGAIN, REFLECT ON
THE PARTY OR DINNER AHEAD.

YOU ARE ALL SET,
READY TO ENJOY YOUR OWN
SOIRÉE. GREET YOUR GUESTS!

"Wherever you stand,
be the soul of that place."
—Rumi

MUSIC

Music is key to a successful gathering. Be it a party, somewhat loud, to encourage dancing. Be it a sit-down meal, much softer, like Billie Holiday or classical. The tunes should fit the mood of the setting. In a perfect world, have your music chosen before things begin so you are not having to stress about it while the event is underway. Use CDs or a streaming service. Head to my daily blog at TedKennedyWatson.com and click on the *TKW's Spotify Playlist* link. There are a variety of playlists that I made just for you!

COCKTAIL PARTY NO. 1, 2 & 3
Think Ella and Eartha and Chet, Edith, Pink Martini, and Madeleine.

DINNER PARTY NO. 1, 2 & 3
Miles, Dizzy, Duke, Thelonious, and Blossom Dearie set the mood.

PARTY NO. 1, 2 & 3
Where Madonna, Chaka, and the Pet Shop Boys get you moving.

CLASSICAL NO. 1, 2 & 3
Mozart, Handel, Bach, and opera arias will set the stage.

BEING A STELLAR GUEST

RESPOND TO THE INVITATION PROMPTLY.

ARRIVE ON TIME.

BRING A COOL GIFT.

ASK IF HELP IS NEEDED AFTER YOU
HAVE SECURED YOUR COCKTAIL.

MINGLE.

ASK QUESTIONS WHEN MINGLING.

COMPLIMENT THE COOK.

DON'T MONOPOLIZE THE CONVERSATIONS.

BE ONE OF THE FIRST TO DEPART.

SEND A HANDWRITTEN NOTE OF
THANKS TO THE HOST WITHIN A DAY
OR TWO OF THE SWELL EVENT.

TO DINE

SETTING A STYLISH TABLE

———

To me, **A STYLISH TABLE IS WHERE EACH ITEM SHINES ON ITS OWN,** from the plates to the glassware, utensils, and napkins—what I think of as the basics, though they are not basic at all. Then you start adding the extras—oh, they should be stunning! Think of them as jewelry for the table. Flowers, candles (always unscented), interesting objects, truly, whatever makes your heart sing. Our friend Jane gave me a set of dominos she'd hand painted for my birthday. The dominos were each painted a singular color. I was struck by the creativity of the gift. I like them so much that I often use one or a few dotted here and there on a table I put together, picking out the primary color of the vignette. **THEY SPARK CONVERSATION.** That gift even began my collection of vintage dominos.

Setting a stylish table makes your guests excited to get to the table to see everything. End result: the table should make you happy. Walk away for a bit; when you walk back, the table should make you smile.

MIX AND MATCH if you don't have enough place settings for your all your guests. Just try to use things in the same color family—or not. You get to decide. If you have a stunning vintage set from family, use it. Often. A weeknight supper with friends can be just as special as a holiday meal. Use the good stuff!

FLOWERS SHOULD BE LOW so your guests can see one another. Or taller stems quite skinny so they don't block the view. I love using really tall French tulips in single-stem vases running down the middle of the table—sometimes in a straight line; other times dotted around. Most often, I use one type of flower and a good number of them. There is strength in numbers.

PLACE CARDS—in a perfect world, yes. It is a nice way to be in control of where folks sit. But don't sweat it if you don't. Sometimes it's fun to just see where everyone ends up. If we do use place cards, often we tell guests they have to find a new spot at the table for dessert. It mixes things up. For the place card, get creative. Use old Scrabble pieces to spell out a name or initials. Or write a name on a hydrangea or fig leaf at each setting.

WE ALMOST ALWAYS PLATE FOOD for guests and then serve. If it is super casual, we set the platters of food on a side table or in the kitchen on the counter for people to serve themselves. I did a TV segment on the Hallmark channel's *Home & Family*. The table there was a good size to set things out, but not huge. The number one comment received online was, "You did not leave room on the table for the food." If your table is big enough, by all means set the food there. We usually end up having so much other stuff on the table that there is just not room for platters or bowls. Plus, I think the table looks nicer without the serving dishes of food.

TABLE SETTING 101

Setting a table is much like getting dressed. You put your dress or pants on, which for the table is a tablecloth or place mats. Or if you are really in the mood, it could be your birthday suit, and not use either. Then belts and shoes. For the table, that would be the plates and glassware. The silverware is like your everyday jewelry—a watch or ring. Now you are ready to walk out the door. But wait! How boring would that be? Now the fun part begins. A scarf or tie will add a bit of jauntiness to your outfit. For the table, a beautiful napkin will add that bit of flair. If you place stunning candlesticks and objects from near and far on the table, those are like a big statement necklace or other piece of jewelry for your outfit. The flowers become your spritz of perfume or cologne. It is all about layering. Much like getting yourself dressed, you might try something and not like it. Absolutely fine. Try something else. Your eye and your heart will tell you when it is just right. Then you are done! Setting a table should bring you a spark of joy. While setting the table, think of the friends or family soon to be sitting around it, the stories and laughter. Let that fill you with tremendous satisfaction.

TABLE SETTING PREP

Take the time to set out your table settings before you arrange them on the table. Enjoy the process. Much like setting your clothes out on the bed in the morning as you are getting ready for the day. Maybe different glasses would be better? Maybe the bamboo silverware instead of the blue handles? One vase of hydrangeas or two? By setting things out, it allows you to see things as a cohesive whole, which will make the table setting process more enjoyable and efficient.

anatomy of
SETTING A TABLE

1. Tablecloth or Place Mats
2. Plates
3. Glassware
4. Silverware
5. Napkins
6. Salt & Pepper Holders
7. Candles
8. Flowers
9. Eye Candy Objects

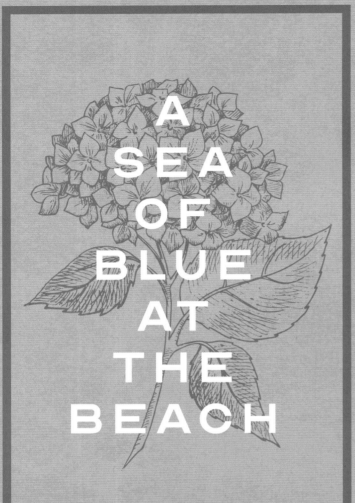

A SEA OF BLUE AT THE BEACH

The hydrangeas set the tone for this alfresco table on the deck, where we can watch the boats sail by. We bring out the dining table the moment the weather starts to turn sunny in the spring. It gets moved around, depending on the size of the guest list. Sometimes it is the dining table; other times it becomes the buffet table.

TED'S TIP
№ 2

When setting a cheery table, choose one color and run with it. Right down to the flowers.

how to: SET A FESTIVE TABLE

FIND OUT EACH GUEST'S FAVORITE FLOWER AND PUT ONE BLOOM
OF THAT IN A SINGLE-STEM VASE AT THEIR PLACE SETTING.

SPELL OUT THE NAMES OF GUESTS IN SCRABBLE TILES AS PLACE CARDS.

USE A FAVORITE SCARF AS A RUNNER OR TABLECLOTH AND TELL THEM
STORY OF WHERE YOU FOUND IT AS THE OPENING STORY TO THE MEAL.

FILL OLD, INTERESTING BOTTLES WITH SPARKLING WATER AND DOT
THEM AROUND THE TABLE FOR FOLKS TO SERVE THEMSELVES.

PLACE A POEM ABOUT FRIENDSHIP UNDERNEATH ONE OF THE
DINING CHAIRS. HAVE THE GUESTS CHECK TO SEE WHO HAS
THE POEM. THE PERSON WHO DOES HAS TO READ IT ALOUD;
THEN PRESENT THEM WITH A SWEET LITTLE GIFT.

SERVE A BELOVED WINE YOU FIRST DISCOVERED ON A
MEMORABLE TRIP. BEFORE YOU DO THE TOAST, TELL A
LITTLE STORY ABOUT THE WINE AND THE TRIP.

ON TRIPS, START A COLLECTION OF SMALL VESSELS. USE THEM
TO HOLD TEA LIGHTS OR VOTIVES AND SCATTER THEM ABOUT
THE TABLE. THE MORE, THE BETTER IN THIS CASE. THERE
CAN NEVER BE TOO MUCH CANDLELIGHT ON THE TABLE.

AFTER DESSERT HAS BEEN
ENJOYED, PASS AROUND A
PLATTER WITH ORANGES AND
WHOLE WALNUTS WITH A NUT
CRACKER, AS WELL AS A DISH
OF CHOCOLATES FOR GUESTS
TO END THE MEAL WITH A
FINAL SWEET FLOURISH.

A COUNTRY SUPPER

If I can't make it to my favorite flower vendor or we don't make it to the Hudson Farmers Market, grocery store blooms often become the easiest flower options when in the country. Here, bunches of vibrant yellow roses clipped super short and propped in drinking glasses are flanked by a clear vessel filled with lemons. The bag of lemons was calling out to me in the produce aisle when I was perusing the roses in the flower section. The big hits of yellow add to the table in the simplest of ways.

there's more

Pair up cheeses with
jams and honey for
interesting flavor
combinations.

I like to use simple white platters for
offering cheeses. Guests are greeted
with it when they arrive, while we
make them a cocktail. The trays are
also easy to pass during the meal.

TO TABLECLOTH,

I personally love a naked table.

There, I said it. The wood grain, the simplicity of it all. In our apartment in Seattle, we have a 100–year-old French fruitwood table (gracing many of these pages) that most times we leave bare. While sitting at it, we will often dream up scenarios of the meals enjoyed at the table by past owners. Or think of all the work done at the table in its lifetime. I often use it as a desk when I want to spread out my paperwork.

But a tablecloth can be lovely too. The feel of the cotton or linen against your skin. The pattern of the fabric adding another layer of interest. A tablecloth absolutely speaks of a fancier table. Bottom line: it is up to you and there is no right or wrong answer. If you feel more comfortable without one, then by all means, run free! If you crave the beauty and comfort of a cloth, then, by all means, use one. My only request: please make sure it is ironed or pressed—which can be a big deterrent for having one; hence, my love of a bare table.

Which brings us to place mats. Rarely have I met a place mat I did not like. A cool place mat is a thing of beauty, adding another texture to a table. Plus, collecting place mats is fun, and they instantly change the look and feel of a table.

Here we used matching tablecloths and brought in an extra table we store in the basement for larger gatherings. This was for our annual Boxing Day supper with family, which we host each year at Hawthorne. We hand carried a box of salmon from the Pike Place Market on the airplane from Seattle to New York for the meal. Our tradition is to fly to the Hudson Valley on Christmas Day after a super busy season at the shops.

OR NOT

things to use as A TABLE COVER

COLORFUL SCARVES

PAGES FROM FALLING-APART VINTAGE BOOKS

WRAPPING PAPER

THIN, COLORFUL VINTAGE BLANKET

PIECE OF COOL OLD FABRIC

HEIRLOOM LINEN BEDDING COVERLETS

EUROPEAN NEWSPAPERS

An oversized scarf with birds flying about becomes the tablecloth. From there, I pulled out the colors of the birds when choosing the tableware, right down to the orange boxes of Louis Sherry truffles. This table became be the inspiration for the one I set for the *Home & Family* show in Los Angeles.

ALL ABOUT
THE FIGS

Our friend Catherine, being the floral maestro that she is, has a sprawling garden. In that beautiful garden on the hillside leading up to her family's home are divine fig trees. She often brings me gifts from the garden. This fig-inspired table was just a matter of laying the fig branches about the dinnerware. Nothing fancy, but oh, such a delight for the eye. The little green figs dancing here and there have a certain magical effect. Each guest got to take home a branch, which made cleanup a breeze.

MENU

SAUVIGNON BLANC

CHICKEN WITH MEYER LEMONS, OLIVES & ROSEMARY (P. 178)

PARMESAN SMASHED POTATOES (P. 182)

MIXED GREENS WITH SHALLOT VINAIGRETTE (P. 183)

[Listen to Dinner Party No. 1 playlist on Spotify at TedKennedyWatson.com]

FIG LEAF CHEESE PLATTER

For weeknight meal, guests arrived and we instantly sat at the dining table and started chatting away. Along with the fig branch–laden table, a wooden cutting board held a hunk of blue cheese and crackers atop an oversized leaf. We passed that around the table as we enjoyed a glass of wine before the chicken came out of the oven.

DISH TOWELS AS OVERSIZED NAPKINS

I love an oversized napkin. Love, love, love. Positively perfect for when you are eating a somewhat . . . actually, make that a really . . . messy meal. Think shrimp boil or fried chicken, either outside or in. My go-to is pretty dish towels instead of smaller napkins. They work great on your lap and the extra size comes in mighty handy. We often drape them over the back of the chairs when setting the table alfresco. That way, guests know something extra tasty is on the menu. It visually whets their appetites for what is ahead. Dish towels are built for heavy use, so a quick wash afterward and they are just like new. To bump up the quality quotient, iron them before setting the table. You want the dish towels to look just as nice as a normal-sized, beautiful napkins, just bigger.

Folded vintage red-checked dish towels from England on the plate at each place setting work perfectly for the messy meal that awaits at WestWard.

THE CHIPPED PLATE

The chip on this plate represents so much of how I feel about the meaning of this book. About my life philosophy, really. That something can have a chip on it but still be absolutely beautiful. We have had a big stack of these simple plates that we have used pretty much daily for close to 30 years. They go in and out of the dishwasher, or sometimes get washed by hand. We use them for all three meals of the day. We use them for when we have company over and I want to set an easy table. The chipped plate lives in the line-up, and I look at it as a good omen when I get it at my place setting. A little flaw that shows what a loved life that plate has lived. Oh, the culinary yummy stuff that has sat atop it. All the laughter it has been present for. All the stories it has heard. All the stories it could tell. While many would have discarded this plate long ago, we see the history of our lives in it. Life certainly is not perfect, but it is pretty darn grand, flaws and all.

EXTRA SEATING

Standing at a party is expected; if you can grab a spot to sit for a bit, lovely. But for brunches and other food-centered gatherings, having a place to sit is vital. That is where extra seating comes in. Folding chairs and chairs you have stashed in your walk-in closet, garage, or basement come in mighty handy in such situations. They certainly don't have to be fancy, but they absolutely can be. One of our friends has a large back stock of Louis Ghost chairs that she often uses for big gatherings. We are huge fans of the classic, stackable Chiavari chairs. At Hawthorne we have a large stack of wood-slat folding chairs that we bought for a song at an antique store. They were used at church functions. We store them in the basement and have used them time and again. A friend in Brooklyn stashes folding chairs under all the beds in his brownstone. You get mighty creative. But, boy, will your guests be happy you did.

A SUNPORCH

MENU

MIMOSA

DUNGENESS
CRAB, CORN &
WHITE CHEDDAR
FRITTATA (P. 180)

HERB ROASTED
POTATOES

ARUGULA SALAD
WITH VEUVE
CLICQUOT
VINAIGRETTE
(P. 183)

BARTLETT HOUSE
SEEDED BREAD

BRUNCH

Using tables to dine at in other rooms than just the dining room or kitchen expands your repertoire tremendously. It also adds a coziness to the meal. Our window-laden front sunporch becomes such a room, and we head to it every chance we can when a table for four is needed.

HOUSE WINE

We started offering a house wine over thirty years ago. Not long out of college, we loved to entertain but were always very conscious about watching how much money we spent. We had been out at a restaurant celebrating a friend's birthday when we had a lovely wine that was not crazy expensive. I took note of the name and hunted it down a few days later. It was super inexpensive with a stellar label. We would buy it by the case. **PRO TIP: IF YOU CAN SWING IT, BUY A CASE.** You are almost always given a good discount when you do. We were off and running with our first house wine! House wine can be inexpensive, right in the middle, or expensive. You decide. The main thing is that you really like it and have enough of it around to offer it liberally to guests. The wine should be easy to drink while you are chatting away as well as when you serve it with food. It is just nice to know you have a go-to wine at the ready that, as Moira Rose would say, is quite potable. It can be red, white or rosé. Or you can do a different house wine of each variety. The idea is to make it your own. It adds an extra-special vibe to something that can be ordinary. I have always loved the phrase "make the ordinary extraordinary." To up the ante and make it even more stylish and memorable, serve it in a decanter. Cheers to house wine!

It is important, and actually fun, to name your home, be it a studio apartment or grand castle. Both hold equal importance in my mind. It is your home, so make it as special as you possibly can. For entertaining, it makes monogramming a cool option, where you can match the lettering with your tableau--on napkin or glassware. The options are unlimited. A house name also provides creative options when sending out invitations. "Drinks at Hawthorne at 7" has a nice ring to it, right? Choose a name that has some meaning to you or just tickles your fancy.

favorite host gifts
TO GIVE <u>AND</u> RECEIVE

A VINTAGE TOKEN FOUND ON YOUR TRAVELS.

A FAVORITE CANDLE OF THE MOMENT. I NEVER TIRE OF GIVING OR RECEIVING THEM.

A SMALL PIECE OF ART PICKED UP AT A SCHOOL AUCTION.

AN INTOXICATING ROOM SPRAY. ONE SPRITZ IN THE AIR CAN TAKE YOU ON A JOURNEY.

A HARD-TO-FIND BOTTLE OF WINE WITH YOUR NAME AND DATE MARKED ON THE BOTTLE IN GOLD INK TO BE REMEMBERED WHEN IT'S ENJOYED.

A SET OF MONOGRAMMED COCKTAIL NAPKINS. YOU CAN NEVER HAVE ENOUGH COCKTAIL NAPKINS.

A BOOK OF POETRY ABOUT FRIENDSHIP THAT YOU INSCRIBE.

A BOX OF GREETING CARDS AND POSTCARDS COLLECTED FROM JOURNEYS NEAR AND FAR.

AN HEIRLOOM HYDRANGEA SENT AFTER THE PARTY.

A BOUQUET OF SCENTED GERANIUM STEMS. SIMPLE AND CHIC ALL AT ONCE.

A SET OF GLASSES IN THE HOST'S FAVORITE COLOR.

A SET OF WHIMSICAL NAPKIN RINGS.

A BOTTLE OF GROVE 45 EXTRA VIRGIN OLIVE OIL. I THINK IT IS THE ABSOLUTE BEST, AND THE BOTTLE IS EXTRAORDINARY TOO.

A FRENCH ZIG ZAG WINE BOTTLE OPENER.

A PAIR OF TIFFANY & CO. CHAMPAGNE FLUTES.

A PLATTER OF HOMEMADE COOKIES. THE PLATTER BECOMES PART OF THE GIFT TOO!

A CANDLE SNUFFER AND A BOX OF COOL MATCHES.

A CELLO BAG FILLED WITH GORGEOUS RADISHES, ALONG WITH A BOX OF AMAZING SEA SALT AND A BRICK OF IRISH BUTTER.

AN ORCHID IN A BEAUTIFUL CACHEPOT.

A BOX OF STATIONERY WITH THE HOST'S NAME OR HOUSE NAME ON IT.

TREATS FROM YOUR FAVORITE BAKERY WRAPPED UP IN A BEAUTIFUL FRENCH DISH TOWEL.

A BIG BUNDLE OF HEAVENLY SCENTED CARNATIONS IN A VINTAGE WATER GLASS.

SAME FLOWERS, TWO WAYS

2

These deep, deep red peonies stopped me in my tracks when I was doing my Saturday stroll through the Pike Place Market flower stalls before opening up the shop at ten. I knew they would look grand with the vintage Spode plates. We had guests both Sunday and Monday for supper and used the same settings both nights, but I played with the flowers a bit to mix it up. They look so different depending on the vessel used.

A DANCING POPPY TABLE

Often, one thing can be the inspiration for setting a table. Here, it is actually two, but they become one. Many years ago at one of my favorite antique malls, I stumbled upon the test tube holders. I loved everything about it and knew instantly that it was coming home with me. It would hold flower stems for a spectacular table. We have enjoyed it flower-less for many years, until I filled it with these divine poppies. They were the starting point for this Veuve dinner with friends in town. The orange from the flowers and the Champagne bottles plus the pink from some of the other blooms became the theme for the tableau. A huge silk scarf became the tablecloth. Orange and pink seersucker napkins were called into action. Tins of Louis Sherry chocolate truffles were take-home gifts for guests to remember the evening, along with the cork from each person's individual bottle of bubbly. By pulling from the colors of the flowers for everything on the table, it became a cohesive whole, which was easy on the eyes.

MENU

VEUVE CLICQUOT

HALIBUT WITH LEMON
& HERBS (P. 190)

SHAVED ASPARAGUS WITH
IRISH BUTTER & PARMESAN

JASMINE RICE WITH
SAUTEED SHALLOTS

DINNER IN TOWN AT THE GAINSBOROUGH

These are the same table, the first occasion, a cozy dinner for deux on Friday night. The next night, a celebratory supper for friends.

LIVE TODAY IN ALL CAPS

Bobeche: a collar on a candle socket, candlestick or chandelier to catch wax drippings

I have been using pages from falling-apart old books as bobeches for as long as I can remember, loving the look and feel of them. It is an easy way to add a bit of visual interest to something that is quite utilitarian. Opt for tall tapers that last a good, long while, or at least for the duration of the meal. Just make sure the candles get blown out before the flame gets close to the paper. Trust me on this tip born from experience.

THE ART OF MIX

Mixing and matching things for your dining table can come from necessity if you find yourself in the spot of not having enough of one thing to fill out each place setting. Or it can come from creativity. Or both. This is where I like to work in pairs. If you have six guests coming but have only four matching plates, then try a pair for the remaining two, and place them across from each other in the middle of the table. Or maybe you have six matching silverware sets but need to set the table for eight. Have a second "pair" be at the heads of the table. It will be a creative look, as if you meant it that way. This formula applies to place settings, glassware, silverware, and napkins. The main takeaway of mix & match is to have the look and feel of it be on purpose, that you have given it some thought. Many of my mix & match tables have ultimately been some of my most favorite, as **CREATIVITY LED THE WAY.**

This table at WestWard on a stellar August eve had me in mix & match heaven. We have a collection of pairs of plates. This provides tons of options for when it is just the two of us for a meal. I thought it would be fun to play with them on the table all at the same time. The chairs are also a mix. The unifying elements are the painted whale glasses and the bamboo cutlery, as well as the striped napkins and Lucite knot rings around them.

& MATCH

TED'S TIP
№ 5

Antique stores, flea markets, tag sales— all are great places to start a silverware collection. You never have to worry about full sets when setting inspired mix & match tables.

MIX & MATCH SILVERWARE

I am in the business of selling tableware, and even *we* don't always have the right number of matching silverware when I go to set a table for a large gathering. This is where the beauty of mixing and matching comes in. A stylish table by no means needs to have everything matching. Quite the opposite. The coolest tables I see in books and magazines, or the ones I set, often have a bit of mixing going on, be it the chairs, napkins, plates, or silverware. If you have eight of a certain pattern and have ten people for supper, set both heads of the table with another set of complementary silverware. That way the middle matches and the ends match. It will be a symmetry that is pleasing to the eye. Or start collecting individual pieces of silverware. It is one of my favorite things we sell at Watson Kennedy. We have big glass jars filled with vintage silverware that we sell by the piece. Folks buy one or many. It warms my heart to think of the gloriously unique tables they will be creating, where every setting is different.

LUNCH IN THE LIVING ROOM

Moving the dining table around to different rooms gives you tons of creative options. Here, the living room becomes the scene. After the meal, you can easily turn it into a game table for a spirited round of cards.

MENU

CHARDONNAY

ASPARAGUS & GRUYÈRE TART (P. 187)

CHILLED CUCUMBER SOUP

LINGUINI WITH ROASTED TOMATOES, BASIL & GARLIC

WATERMELON, FETA & AGED BALSAMIC

[Listen to Classical No. 1 playlist on Spotify at TedKennedyWatson.com]

CLEAR VOTIVE HOLDERS

These are basics that come in handy, basically, every time we entertain, both big and small. Clear glass votive holders are go-tos for little beautiful hits of light here and there. Use unscented white votives so you can use tons of them if you wish, with no fear of over-scenting a table, room, or party. **SCATTER THEM EVERYWHERE.** You will be happy you did. You don't have to worry about dripping, which is a concern with tapers and pillars. Votives are inexpensive. Look to restaurant supply stores for cases of them—both the glass holders and the candles. We always have several boxes at the ready. Bonus: if the power ever goes out, we are all set! For a party, run them down the food table and have them at the bar, on side tables, on window ledges, in the bathroom—you name it.

TED'S TIP
Nº 6

Count how many candles you light at the start of the event and write that number down. Trust me on this one. After a hunt-and-gather expedition around your home to blow them all out, you will sleep much easier if you know exactly how many you lit to start with.

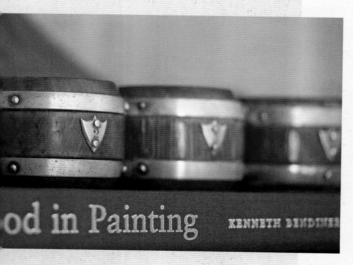

BUYING NAPKINS & NAPKIN RINGS

Napkins for the table or cocktail table are an easy way to add a stylish flourish. In my mind, you can never have enough napkins. Whether it's cotton or linen napkins for the dining table or packs of cocktail napkins for drinks, the more the merrier. Always be on the lookout—at housewares stores like mine, antique and thrift stores, in catalogs, and from online vendors. Solid colors and wonderful patterns for mixing and matching. Having a lovely assortment on hand makes setting a table a joy. Buy one or many. One lone napkin can become an instant favorite for yourself when you have a meal solo. Two for when it is just you and a friend or spouse. People so often think they have to buy twelve of one type of napkin. Not true. Keep napkins freshly laundered and folded neatly in a drawer or closet so you can access easily.

Using napkins is an easy way to add tons of style and lots of color and pattern to even the simplest of tables. Start a collection! When out and about shopping, if a set catches your eye, snap it up. Sets of two, four, six, eight. Don't always feel like you have to buy a large number, which can be quite costly. If your family is primarily you and your mate, concentrate on finding pairs. Look for cotton or linen options that have a nice weight to them and will launder well. While I have no problem ironing up a grouping of napkins for guests, we use cloth napkins at each meal, so I search for ones that look great right out of the dryer. Add napkin rings to your list when you're on the hunt. Like picking out a ring from the jewelry box, a little bit of bling adds a bit of wow!

setting up
a stylish dining table: CITY

1. Polished silverware
2. Lots of votive candles
3. Low blooms or single stems scattered down the middle of the dining table
4. Pressed napkins in napkin rings
5. Individual salt & pepper cellars at each setting
6. Bring out your best china and flutes

MENU

FRENCH 75 (P. 171)

SHRIMP, PEAS & MINT RISOTTO (P. 192)

MIXED GREENS WITH BLOOD ORANGE VINAIGRETTE

FRAN'S SALTED CARAMELS

Listen to
Dinner Party No. 2
playlist on Spotify at
TedKennedyWatson.com

GLASSWARE

Oh, my stars, where do I even begin to start when addressing glassware? It could be said that I never passed on a glass that caught my eye. We have a large assortment at each of our homes, bringing us tons of happiness every time we reach to make a drink. Buy glasses in really any number. Having a solo glass can make you feel extra special. Having stacks of one type when you throw a party or host a large dinner can make you feel extra fancy. A variety of glassware is a fun collection to grow and pull from to set a stylish table. Mix and match. Not all glasses on the table have to be part of a set. If you are just starting out, begin with clear. They are the most versatile to work with. Then branch out and start adding color to your repertoire. **YOU WILL START TO FEEL A LITTLE RUSH OF GLEE** once you start reaching for glasses when setting the table. Glasses can be the little extra flourish that makes the table sing.

The true secret of happiness lies in taking a genuine interest in all the details of daily life.
—William Morris

BIRTHDAY
TABLE IN GREENS

A table for four with dear friends to fête the birthday of TPS. The French lettuce plate was the starting point for this table. I sent baker extraordinaire Elizabeth Mayhew in Millbrook a photo of said plate. She worked her magic, creating a carrot cake that was a showstopper. Often, one element can be the driving force behind a tablescape. It could be a color, an object, or an idea floating around in your brain that you want to bring to life. I say, "Have fun with it!"

Happiness is not having what you want. It is appreciating what you have.

MENU

CABERNET SAUVIGNON

SPARKLING WATER

STUFFED CHICKEN BREAST WITH CRACKED BLACK PEPPER CHÈVRE (P. 185)

CORN DUTCH BABY (P. 184)

CARROT CAKE BIRTHDAY CAKE

HOME & FAMILY

So, there we were, pulling into the Universal lot, Bailey on my lap, signing in to head to the set for the show. TPS was driving around all these sets we recognized from movies and TV shows over the years. Kind of a riot. The *Home & Family* set is actually a house, each room a stage set for individual segments. While one segment is being shot, another is being set up. At least thirty folks are buzzing around getting things ready and ultimately shooting each segment. It is all highly organized and orchestrated.

Erika from the shop flew down to help me, as each and every thing on that table had to be unpacked in a quick amount of time. I would set most of the table before cameras started rolling. Then a quick trip into hair and makeup to get camera ready. The host for my segment was Cameron Mathison. Such a nice guy, he instantly made me feel relaxed. We had a fun banter while setting up the rest of the table while the cameras were rolling. Let's just say six minutes goes by in the blink of an eye. Six minutes turned into nine. I get quite passionate about my table settings!

No act of kindness,
no matter how small,
is ever wasted.
—Aesop

AN ISLAND SHRIMP BOIL

Click on the QR icon to see how to make this one-pot wonder for your next gathering. Outside or indoors, it is sure to be a hit.

A shrimp boil is a festive, hands-on, easy way to entertain a group of folks for a meal.

It's a one-pot supper that can feed a crowd. Newspapers spread out on the table instantly make an interactive party feel, and guests know they are in for a treat. This is where oversized napkins are a must. The meal is indeed meant to be finger-licking good. An ice-cold beer, G&T, or a glass of rosé is perfect with shrimp boil in every way. Cleanup is a breeze—just gather the newspapers and the work is done.

BRUNCH MENU

BAGELS & LOX WITH CREAM CHEESE

CHOPPED LIVER

ROASTED NEW POTATOES

**FRUIT SALAD MEDLEY STUDDED
WITH POMEGRANATE SEEDS**

MIMOSAS

COFFEE

[Listen to
Classical No. 2
playlist on Spotify at
TedKennedyWatson.com]

*Having friends over for a Sunday
brunch in town is a great way to
catch up and entertain a crowd.*

WEEKNIGHT MENU

ROAST CHICKEN (HOME COOKED, FROM A FAVORITE
RESTAURANT, OR A GROCERY STORE ROTISSERIE)

ZUCCHINI & POTATO TIAN (P. 179)

COOKIE ASSORTMENT FROM NEIGHBORHOOD BAKERY

HOUSE RED WINE

SPARKLING WATER

A SIMPLE TABLE TWO WAYS

We look for every opportunity we can to dine outside. Often that means back-to-back entertaining from one day to the next. When this happens, I like to use the same tablecloth and flowers to make it easier but mix it up a bit by swapping out different glassware and napkins and such.

Here, the long picnic table out back at Hawthorne is getting a workout. The simplest table with plain white plates and clear glassware is set for a picnic-style lunch.

Next it is set for an early supper, where freshly planted lavender joins the lilacs, and the table gets a bit more color with the addition of green glassware, silverware, napkin rings, and seersucker napkins.

LUNCHEON MENU

ROSÉ

PAPPARDELLE WITH GARLICKY,
LEMONY SHRIMP & FETA

BAGUETTE WITH SALTED FRENCH BUTTER

TATE'S GINGER COOKIES

COFFEE & TEA

AN EASY LUNCH

Attention is the rarest and purest form of generosity. —Weil

Being a good host does not always have to mean throwing a party or large dinner. Sometimes it is just having lunch with a friend at your home. Could not be simpler. I like to put out the platter of dessert as part of the table setting, this time hazelnut and chocolate cookies from our favorite French bakery and peak-of-the-season cherries. No baking required! For the meal, a salad with a big dollop of homemade tuna salad on top. With a basket of really good crackers and a glass of white wine, you are all set to catch up with an old friend.

FRIDAY NIGHT PIZZA & MARTINIS

We have been having friends over for pizza and martinis on Friday nights for as long as I can remember.

WE LOVE THE HIGH/LOW OF IT ALL, the simplicity of pizza served with a martini in a chic glass. It is also one of the easiest things to do on a weeknight. I mean, seriously. We set out a big bowl of truffled popcorn or an easy appetizer board, make folks a martini, and catch up while we wait for the pizza and salad to be delivered. I always set the table in the morning before heading to the shop. We get home, I light a bunch of candles, TPS feeds and walks Bailey, and by the time they get back, we are ready to greet guests. Dessert is something simple like vanilla bean ice cream with Fran's caramel sauce. The dinner party could not be easier. Sometimes it is a few friends, sometimes it is quite a few. It is a super easy way to host and see your friends when life is busy.

For friends who arrive early, a hearty appetizer board is a great way to have a few hearty bites before the pizza is delivered. Cheese is a major component to the evening. I will often heavily pepper a log of plain chèvre to bump up the flavor. Besides, I like the way the pepper looks on the board. To balance that, a scattering of chunky French salt to go with the radishes. A big dollop of stone ground mustard is a nice accompaniment to the cheeses.

USING WHAT YOU HAVE

Setting a table is an activity **WHERE CREATIVITY AND RESOURCE-FULNESS ARE OFTEN THE DRIVING FORCES.** I also know from talking to many, many customers, it is a task that can bring on much apprehension and a tiny bit of fear to many. Some of my most interesting "tablescaping" has been out of pure necessity, when we have been out on the island or in the country and everything is closed for a holiday, and I had to look at objects around the house in a different way. My biggest piece of advice here is to take a deep breath and walk around your home or yard, getting inspired. Pluck off those cool-looking branches. Use a cherished piece of silver that has been deep in a drawer. Go through your closet and choose a scarf as a tablecloth. Our first supper at our home in New York was literally the night we closed on the property. I used hydrangea leaves all over the table, as very few blooms had yet begun. Vases were old bottles left behind by the lovely previous owner. We had an old green domino set, so I scattered the pieces about. There are no rules. Use what you have and let your creative spirit soar.

SEEING
RED

Red is such a passion-filled color. I use it as often as possible. For this table, the little streaks of red in the creamy tulips were the inspiration. That is all it takes, **JUST ONE LITTLE THING TO SPARK YOUR IMAGINATION.** Then let it run wild! The Italian cookie tin screamed at me as I was walking around the house pulling things for this table vignette. Pick me, pick me! It would be the perfect vessel to hold those insanely beautiful tulips. Then I start layering. As I have said before, like getting dressed. Put something on the table; if you don't love how it looks, move on to the next option. Then you add another thing. Then another. By choosing one color it limits your choices, but that also makes it easier when choosing objects. Plus, it creates an instantly visual treat for your guests when they first lay their eyes on it.

The sweetest of sweet peas . . .

A SWEET GIFT

Often, I do one **vase of flowers** at each **place setting**.

Then after the meal and the evening has ended, guests get to take the arrangement home in the vessel. We collect vintage bottles and glasses, so it becomes a remembrance of the gathering long after the blooms have faded.

HERB
BOUQUETS

The hand-tied little herb bouquets were made for us by the amazing Forest Garden Farm on Vashon Island. They were loved by all throughout the meal and then everyone got to take one home to enjoy in their cooking for the coming weeks. It is these little touches that make your gatherings memorable long after the dinner party has ended.

LAYERING A TAB

We received a variety of flowers the week this table was set. In an homage to the friendship those blooms represented, we got to enjoy them at every meal we sat at the table. They were the starting point for the layering; then an old match striker picked up in London along with candlesticks bought at Tail of the Yak in Berkeley. A Cire Trudon candle and little boxes made out of hollowed-out tree branches. Chunky place mats at the ready for an evolving round of plates and glassware. At the end of the table an assortment of brass candlesticks and a large cloche. **EVERYWHERE YOUR EYE LANDS, IT'S TREATED TO SOMETHING INTERESTING.**

LE

A thick, woven place mat over a hand-block-printed tablecloth instantly adds layering to the table. The fluttery yellow tulips having an almost peony vibe to them.

WHAT IS A NIBBLE?

I prefer to use the term *nibbles* over *hors d'oeuvre* for a host of reasons. The first is the spelling. I think I am a reasonably good speller, but the H word always has me searching on Google for the proper spelling. Secondly, I do think the H word has a place, but I think of it as being more formal, like when food is passed at a cocktail party. Nibbles fit the bill when you are just putting out a quick and easy assortment of things to have with cocktails before dinner. Put out some nibbles, make your guests a drink, and watch the conversation start to flow.

Nibble
Function: noun
Date 1658
1: an act of nibbling.
2: a very small quantity or portion;
also, snack.

SETTING THE TABLE BEFORE YOU LEAVE IN THE MORNING

HAVING A NICE MEAL AT HOME AFTER A LONG WORKDAY IS GOOD FOR THE SOUL, whether it just for you or for having company over. Whether that meal involves ordering takeout or cooking, sitting and enjoying the moment and reflecting on the day is a ritual so many of us enjoy immensely. But setting the table just before can be an added stress. If I know we are going to be a tad later getting home than usual, I like to quickly set the table before we head out the door in the morning. I find it energizes me a bit, thinking of the relaxing supper that awaits when we get home. All that is left is to light the candles, and away we go!

AN AUTUMN ALFRESCO LUNCH

In the Hudson Valley, the month of October is magical beyond words. We grab any chance we can to have friends up from the city and break bread with them at the long, white picnic table just off the back porch. The leaves fall around us as we dine. A yummy French red fills our glasses, a tasty squash soup fills our bellies, and **LAUGHTER AND MANY STORIES FILL THE AIR.**

DON'T FORGET BREAKFAST

Breakfast is a great way to entertain.

IT DOES NOT HAVE TO BE ANYTHING FANCY, and it is often on the shorter time side of events, as folks have to get to work or get on with their weekend activities. Either a weekday or weekend breakfast is a swell way to gather. Make one large dish that can be divided, like a big frittata, so you are not in the kitchen cooking after your guests have arrived. I like to buy really good muffins from our favorite bakery and have coffee and orange juice on the table so folks can help themselves. Set the table the night before. To make it extra special, have a bundle of produce from the farmers market as part of the table setting. It can be the parting gift as guests head out to start their day!

A GIFT SPARKS A TABLE SETTING

Sometimes **ONE THING IS ALL IT TAKES TO SPARK CREATIVITY.** Be it to paint on a canvas, create a stylish room, or set a comfortable table. My friend Kathy drove up from Eugene for the day to see me and do a little shopping. She brought us the loveliest gift of Italian horn-handled flatware from her personal collection. She knew of my fondness for horn, as she had seen me set tables with it for years. I could not wait to get home that night to cook dinner and set the table using the new-old setting. Celebrating, using, and enjoying gifts we receive is of great importance to both of us. So much so for me, it is the business I am in! **IT HONORS AND PAYS HOMAGE TO THE GIVER.**

1

THE TABLE STARTS WITH ONE THING

One thing is all that is needed to get the creative juices flowing. Maybe it's a bundle of tulips, a favorite place setting, even an object from a cherished trip. Then you are off and running. Add, subtract. **KEEP GOING UNTIL YOUR EYE IS PLEASED.** Here a gift from our friend Denise Fiedler is what started my imagination running. An orb created out of silk ribbon. The artist gets into a meditative state while knotting, winding, and creating each one. The white lilacs always find a seat at our table. The season might be short but, boy, is it sweet.

SATURDAY NIGHT SIT-DOWN DINNER MENU

CITRUS BAKED BRIE (P. 188)

SALMON WITH MUSTARD TERIYAKI SAUCE

JASMINE RICE WITH CARAMELIZED SHALLOTS

CAULIFLOWER STEAKS WITH CAPERS, OLIVES & LEMONS (P. 186)

RASPBERRY SORBET WITH CARAMEL SAUCE

WHITE OR A LIGHT RED WINE, SUCH AS MERLOT

Listen to
Dinner Party No. 2
playlist on Spotify at
TedKennedyWatson.com

QUAIL-EGG EASTER TABLE

I think quail eggs are the most magical, beautiful things. Little works of art, really. I love using them as decoration for Easter, by just doting them around the dining table. Here they dance about among the long-stemmed tulips from the Pike Place Market. You could certainly use eggs that you have colored for the occasion. **AGAIN, THERE IS NO RIGHT OR WRONG. USE WHAT PLEASES YOUR EYE.**

A MARTINI

MENU

**MARTINIS
(PG. 168—170)**

**BALSAMIC CHICKEN
& SHALLOTS**

**ARUGULA SALAD
WITH CORN &
CHERRIES**

**CHOCOLATE CHIP—
LADEN BANANA
BREAD (P. 189)**

LUNCH

Lunch on the front sunporch at Hawthorne is always a treat. If it involves good friends and a martini, even better. The scented geranium topiary set the stage for this table, and then I just ran with the green theme. Cheers!

A
HOUSE BEAUTIFUL
LUNCH

Newell Turner, who was the editor-in-chief at the time at *House Beautiful*, asked me to set and shoot a lunch table for an upcoming issue. We had just bought Hawthorne so were not as well stocked as we would normally be. I had to **GET SUPER CREATIVE** using the limited number of things from around the house and property. The limelight hydrangeas were in bloom out front, so they started everything rolling, with green and white being the theme. We found the tablecloth, which was actually just a large piece of fabric that fit the table perfectly, at a vintage shop in Sheffield. We scattered Glassybaby about. My friend Margot hand painted simple, clear glasses with a large H and had Hawthorne painted in full. A John Derian tray from the shop pulled the whole country table vibe together.

SUPPER UNDER THE EAVES

Ahhhhh, the best-laid plans. That is why **A BACKUP PLAN IS VITAL** when entertaining at home. Rain was in the forecast the day of this gathering. Rather than taking a chance, we moved the table under the porch eaves to be certain the meal would go off without a hitch. Literally moments before guests arrived, the rain began. We were all set and ready for it! The peonies were the stars of this table anyway. There was no way the rain was going to upstage them, although the hand-painted swirl plates certainly gave them a run for their money.

RED, WHITE & BLUE

July out on the island when the geraniums are going crazy in their pots is such a treat. I try to work them into table settings whenever possible. It is an easy way to get a flowery hit without breaking the bank. A red-checked vinyl tablecloth that I picked up at the hardware store for a song can be easily wiped down and is perfect for alfresco dining. French dish towels became the place mats, a trick I use often, as I like how they add an extra layer to a table, especially when the meal can be messy. Here, barbeque chicken was on the menu. **THE SOUND OF THE INCOMING TIDE WAS OUR MUSIC FOR THE MEAL.**

When we have a guest from out of town, we love to host a dinner in their honor.

There is something about opening your home and cooking a meal that brings folks together in a relaxed and intimate way. If you know their favorite flower, have it as the centerpiece of the table. It might seem like a small detail but it is one that will not go unnoticed.

LUNCH AMONG THE HERBS

By now, you probably know that I think moving your dining table around
is a very good thing. Think of all the cool spots you have around your home,
both in and out. Setting up the dining table in a different spot from usual
gives you loads of new creative options. Not only will it be a treat for your
guests, but also for you. It gives you a completely different perspective.

THE IVY TABLE

Buying tabletop goods while on your travels is a really special way to remember said trip and the experience of finding the treasures that you are now dining upon. This was certainly the case with these beautiful hand-painted plates from a favorite restaurant of ours in Los Angeles, The Ivy. If you ever find yourself even remotely close, you must go. **IT IS A FEAST FOR THE SENSES.** The flowers, food, drinks, service, and people watching are all sublime. They serve their food on these plates, as well as bowls and platters and jugs. They also sell and ship it. So, when we dine with guests using these plates in Seattle, we are transported a bit. And they make for a fun Los Angeles story with those we are breaking bread with.

THE CHEESEBALL TAKES CENTER STAGE

This is a family recipe our sister-in-law Nan makes pretty much every time we visit. I love how the taste of something can bring back a flood of fond memories.

Think outside the box when it comes to a tablecloth. Here, two French Pierre Frey pillowcases set the tone for this table. I gave them a good ironing and overlapped them, knowing the silver tray, candlesticks, and Henry Dean vessels would cover most of where they overlap.

CHEESEBALL RECIPE

Two 8-ounce packages of cream cheese along with a 5-ounce jar of Old English sharp cheddar spread. All should be left on the counter and brought to room temperature. Add those to a large mixing bowl so you can work in a few generous pinches of garlic powder and a few big shakes of Worcestershire sauce from the bottle. Mix all together. Refrigerate to chill. Over medium stovetop heat, toast up a good amount of broken pecan pieces. Let cool. Once the cheese mixture has chilled, form it into a ball. Roll that in the pecans until it is fully covered.

A FISHY TABLE

The oversized fish dish towel was a gift from friends traveling through Italy. They were coming to supper, so I wanted to incorporate it into the table. I used it as an overlay on the runner. The fish motif became the theme of the table. Shells from the beach used in a clear vase to support the hydrangea stems pulled it all together.

A WELL-TIMED

FARM STAND STOP

The luscious yarrow we picked up at Forest Garden Farm set the tone for this table. They were the only flowers left at the stand and, lucky us, they could not have been more fitting. Looking at the little blooms throughout the meal was an absolute delight.

THE ONE THING YOU HAVE THAT NOBODY ELSE HAS IS YOU. YOUR VOICE. YOUR MIND. YOUR CREATIVITY. YOUR VISION. YOUR STORY. SO, WRITE AND DRAW AND BUILD AND PLAY AND SET AWESOME TABLES AND DANCE AND LIVE AS ONLY YOU CAN.

TO PARTY

HOSTING A PARTY

Hosting a party—be it a small weeknight gathering for drinks, a sit-down dinner, or a big bash—you should enjoy the process. Big or small, hosting a party takes lots of work and a good outlay of dough, and you still have to clean up after everyone has gone. But, if done right, you will have one heck of a swell time at your own party and all that other stuff will just fall from memory once all is said and done. I have used the word "privileged" before, and, again, I mean it in spades here. It is a privilege to host a party of any size. Revel in that. Be honored. Not everyone has the energy or resources or desire. Enjoy every step along the way. What is that saying? "A life well lived is not the destination; it is in the journey"? This rings doubly true when it comes to being the host of a party.

Happy
Party
Memories

BELOVED
BALLOONS

One of my earliest memories is of a birthday party my parents had for me when I was quite young. Little kids from the neighborhood came to the party. My mom had decorated the kitchen with all sorts of festive delights. Each chair was tied with a different color floating balloon. The sight of them joyfully floating above the table is where my love of balloons began. They are happy. They just are. For years, I have incorporated them into parties we have hosted. **BALLOONS CAN MAKE AN ADULT AS GLEEFULLY HAPPY AS THEY CAN A CHILD.** When my first book came out, we had a big book-signing party at one of the Watson Kennedy shops. It has really tall ceilings, and there were tons of green balloons floating around the space at different heights. Green was a predominant color on the front of the book and holds a very special place in my heart.

For my fortieth birthday, Mister Sive threw me a party in the same space. Balloons floated everywhere, with incredibly long streamers dancing about. It was a sea of balloons. What a sight! The party went to the wee hours, and as we departed, we set the alarm as usual, headed home and fell fast asleep. Quite early that morning, I heard my phone ring. It was the alarm company. The alarm was going off. We jumped into the car and headed to the shop, which is a quick twelve blocks away. The balloons had started to deflate, setting off the motion detector. What we found out a bit later is that the alarm had been going off for hours. The alarm company had tried calling many times but we slept right through it. The police came and went, once they realized no one had broken into the building. Our poor neighbors! It is one of many funny memories from that party, and of course, it involved my beloved balloons.

Our home in Seattle
is at The Gainsborough.

Built in 1929, there are four apartments on each floor, each getting a corner.
We bought it not long after we met. We moved away for eleven years shortly
after our fifth anniversary party but kept it, renting it out, as we always knew
we would one day return. It is the scene for both very memorable soirées—
our fifth and twentieth anniversary parties.

5TH ANNIVERSARY

We asked our neighbor if we could use her kitchen so the caterers could work out of there, and we turned our kitchen into the bar. The bartender was set up in there, so guests could head straight to the kitchen after they arrived. The long, French fruitwood dining table became the buffet, getting pushed up against the wall. Balloons with festive streamers filled the space. Votive candles dotted the ledges of every window. Tulips swayed about the tables. Just a handful of years out of college, the volume of the music was just a tad louder than at our 20th anniversary. The apartment was packed with guests: work friends, college friends, family—the perfect mix to celebrate our five years together. Our kitty, Georgia O'Keeffe, meandered about. Some people danced to the music. Small groups huddled together to chat. Toasts were made. Tears were shed. Laughter and love filled the air.

20TH ANNIVERSARY

By this time, we had moved back to the apartment. Our art collection had grown—we have a tradition of giving each other a piece of art for each anniversary—and there was barely an empty spot on the walls. We asked our neighbors, a young couple, if we could put them up for a night at the Inn at the Market, which is where one of my shops is located, in exchange for using their kitchen, as well as storing some pieces of furniture. Fifteen years had passed and the space was stuffed with stuff. Fitting in 100-plus guests would require a bit of creative finesse. We have a dear friend of a friend, Jay, who lived in Portland but had moved to NYC. He had bartended for us before, so we flew him in to work the party. He is always a hit! Food was passed this time, instead of being set out on the buffet. Bailey, our beloved miniature Schnauzer, worked the room. Many of the same folks from our fifth anniversary were there, along with new friends. Our businesses had grown, so there were more folks from each of our fields too. Buckets of tulips from Pike Place Market filled the space. The light from votive candles lit the rooms. The music was a tad softer than fifteen years before. But the love and laughter were deeper and louder. Once again, toasts were made and tears were shed. Milestone parties create indelible memories. The amount of work and expense drifts away, and only the fond memories and stories remain.

GO OLD SCHOOL

Send out invitations in the mail.

Sure, evites are super easy, but nothing beats the mannerly ritual of reaching into a mailbox and pulling out an invitation that has a handwritten name and address on it. Add a meaningful, cool-looking stamp for bonus points. All of it instantly bumps up the specialness quotient of your soirée. Here are a few invites from our early years that kicked off the many years of party-throwing ahead. These are really simple but very personal. That combo beats an evite any day.

Manners mirror the soul.

A
DRINKS
TRAY

A proper drinks tray setup can be a thing of beauty. It can be **A BEACON TO GUESTS UPON ARRIVAL.** A place they can make their own drink while the host is hosting other arrivals. A mix of liquor bottles, mixers, and glasses. A stack of cocktail napkins. Stirrers. Add a bowl of nuts, chips, or popcorn and you are off and running for a fun, festive eve. We like to set up various stations so folks can help themselves. This is particularly helpful for a large party, when the line for a drink is long and the bartender is swamped.

COCKTAIL PARTY TO-DO LIST

SET-UP BAR WITH GLASSES, BOOZE, SODAS, AND SPARKLING WATERS.

MAKE GREEN GODDESS DIP.

ASSEMBLE CHEESE PLATTERS.

FILL UP HOTEL SILVER BOWLS WITH NUTS AND CHIPS.

SET VASES OF FLOWERS ABOUT.

LIGHT TONS OF VOTIVES AND A FEW SCENTED CANDLES.

MAKE SURE THE BATHROOM HAS CLEAN TOWELS, A FULL ROLL OF TOILET PAPER, A FULL BOTTLE OF HAND SOAP, A BOTTLE OF ROOM SPRAY, FRESH FLOWERS, AND A LIT SCENTED CANDLE.

TURN ON PARTY MUSIC.

SET OUT FOOD.

FILL ICE BUCKETS.

START YOUR COCKTAIL, SIT A BIT, AND REVEL AT HOW SWELL YOU ARE.

GREET GUESTS.

HAVE A BLAST AT YOUR OWN PARTY.

anatomy of
A HOME BAR

Choose the perfect spot that guests can easily find—a corner in the living room or kitchen. It should be a location where flow of people is easy and the bartender, if you have hired one, has room to move. One very large tray, or a variety, instantly makes it look stellar. This is, after all, a home bar. **IT SHOULD LOOK INTERESTING**, but you are not trying to emulate the Bar Hemingway at the Ritz Paris. You can also make an entire table the bar. We often do this in our kitchen in town, where we have a butcher block–topped table in the corner. An interesting ice bucket is always a plus. Don't forget the cocktail napkins. I like to set out a bowl of peanuts in the shell. That way guests can have a little project to work on and a nibble while their drink is being made.

1. Gin
2. Vodka
3. Scotch
4. White wine
5. Red wine
6. Tonic
7. Seltzer water
8. 7 Up
9. Lemons
10. Limes
11. Olives
12. Bowl of peanuts in the shell
13. Bowl for shells
14. Cocktail napkins
15. One simple type of clear glass

setting up
AN EXTRA-SPECIAL BAR

**EVERYTHING FROM THE LIST
ON PRIOR PAGE, PLUS:**

1. Rosé wine
2. Tequila
3. Whiskey
4. Tomato juice
5. Italian sodas
6. A variety of glassware
7. Linen cocktail napkins
8. Bowl of cashews
9. Vase of flowers
10. Hire a bartender

VEUVE CLICQUOT MEMORIES

The French Champagne Veuve Clicquot has a very long history in my life. In my shop in downtown Seattle, you will see a quite large, perpetual display of the bottles that were enjoyed for my fortieth and fiftieth birthday parties held at that location. They are two events that are indelibly marked in my brain with pure joy. That Veuve played a large part in the festivities cements my love for it even more. Many years ago, when I had my wholesale showroom, I represented a jewelry artist and we presented her work in Paris at one of the big shows. After each very long day, we would have a lovely supper out and then walk back to Hôtel Le Tourville, stopping along the way at a corner market to pick up a bottle of Veuve. We would sit and enjoy the bubbles in the tiny lobby-lounge where the hotel encouraged guests to bring their own bottle. It is a pretty magical hotel. **UNPRETENTIOUS AND FABULOUS AND COMFY AND STYLISH.** We did this every evening for the duration of our work in Paris. It is where my love affair with the Champagne began. TPS and I went to the house in Reims as part of my fortieth birthday and were treated to a personal tasting. The story of La Grande Dame Veuve Clicquot is legendary. She played a large part in the distribution of Champagne as we know it even to this day. We sell a book on her at Watson Kennedy that has been a bestseller for us. For the first book signing party of my debut book, Veuve played a big part in the festivities.

the easiest
NO-COOK COCKTAIL NIBBLES

I remember once reading about a well-heeled gentleman who said all that was needed to host a good cocktail party was to open a can of peanuts. I loved that. What he was getting at was that folks often fret about what to serve and the amount of work, so they don't invite friends over for drinks. Silly! Here is my list of store-bought goodness that will make you look like a pro without breaking a sweat. **SERVE IN YOUR PRETTIEST BOWLS AND ON YOUR MOST FETCHING PLATTERS.** Then sit back and enjoy your fête!

POTATO CHIPS, IN A BIG SILVER BOWL. SUPER HIGH-LOW. TIM'S AND CAPE COD ARE FAVORITES.

A PIECE OF BEECHER'S FLAGSHIP CHEESE NEXT TO THE BEST CRACKERS YOU CAN FIND.

A BIG WOODEN BOWL OF TRUFFLE-SALTED POPCORN.

A PLATTER WITH AN OPENED TIN OF SARDINES, A DOLLOP OF DIJON MUSTARD, A PILE OF FRENCH CORNICHONS, AND A STACK OF TRISCUITS. (THANK YOU TO CHEF GABRIELLE HAMILTON AT PRUNE. THIS IS OUR GO-TO PARTY SNACK.)

A BOWL FULL OF PITTED CASTELVETRANO OLIVES.

A PLATTER WITH A SLICED BAGUETTE AND A DISH OF TAPENADE.

A SILVER BOWL OF CASHEWS WARMED WITH A SPRIG OF ROSEMARY. YOUR HOME WILL SMELL HEAVENLY.

OPEN-FACED TOMATO SANDWICHES WITH CHERRY TOMATOES, ALONGSIDE A BOWL OF CHUNKY MALDON SEA SALT.

GOLDFISH. JULIA CHILD'S AND MY HUSBAND'S FAVORITE.

PISTACHIOS WITH THE SHELLS ON, WITH A BOWL FOR THE SHELLS NEXT TO THEM.

PECANS WARMED WITH SPRINKLE OF BROWN SUGAR.

OLIVES WITH BOWL FOR THE PITS. A VARIETY OF BOTH SIZE AND COLOR, ALWAYS A LOVELY SIGHT.

CARROT STICKS NEXT TO A DISH OF STORE-BOUGHT HUMMUS.

A PLATTER OF SLICED SALAMI, SLICED CHEDDAR CHEESE, AND A SLICED BAGUETTE.

STORE-BOUGHT PIGS IN A BLANKET—TRUST ME ON THIS ONE—ALONG WITH SMALL BOWLS OF KETCHUP AND MUSTARD.

CAPRESE ON A TOOTHPICK. CHERRY TOMATO, BASIL, AND A SMALL BALL OF MOZZARELLA.

HOSTING A PARTY
ON A WEEKDAY WORK NIGHT

OFFER ONE WINE OPTION—WHITE OR ROSÉ.

OFFER A SIGNATURE COCKTAIL, SUCH AS A NEGRONI OR A G&T.

SERVE A CHEESE TRAY—THREE CHEESES,
ONE JAM, ASSORTED CRACKERS.

SELECT A VARIETY OF NO-COOK NIBBLES FROM PREVIOUS PAGE.

LIGHT CANDLES.

HAVE ON YOUR FAVORITE COCKTAIL
PLAYLIST—ELLA, BILLIE, OR LOUIE.

OR TRY MY SPOTIFY PARTY NO. 3 SELECTION.

HOSTING A FANCY WEEKEND COCKTAIL PARTY

HAVE A FULL BAR.

HIRE A BARTENDER.

A SIGNATURE COCKTAIL ADDS A FESTIVE AIR.

SET FLOWERS OF THE SEASON
IN ALL THE BEST PLACES.

HAVE VOTIVE CANDLES FLICKERING
ABOUT EVERYWHERE.

ENCOURAGE "DRESSY" ATTIRE. IT'S ALWAYS
FUN TO SEE HOW FOLKS INTERPRET THAT!

HAVE A FEW PASSED FOODS, LIKE BACON-
WRAPPED DATES, CHICKEN SKEWERS
WITH PEANUT SAUCE, MEATBALLS, SMOKED
SALMON BLINI, A DOLLOP OF CAVIAR
SERVED ON A POTATO CHIP.

AS HOST, HAVE ONE QUESTION THAT YOU
ASK EACH OF YOUR GUESTS WHILE YOU
ARE CHATTING WITH THEM THROUGH-
OUT THE PARTY. IT'S INTERESTING TO
SEE HOW MUCH THE ANSWERS VARY.

LIVE MUSIC IS A HUGE TREAT IF YOU CAN
SWING IT. A FAB PLAYLIST IS ALWAYS
A GOOD SECOND CHOICE. MY SPOTIFY
PARTY NO. 1 WILL GET FOLKS HOPPING.

*"Sharing is a sign of
love and friendship."
—Jean Imbert*

FESTIVE COCKTAIL PARTY GOODNESS

CAVIAR WITH BLINI OR GO HIGH-LOW WITH TATER TOTS.
SET NEXT TO A BOWL OF CRÈME FRAÎCHE.

NEW POTATOES WITH A BOWL OF GREEN GODDESS DRESSING FOR DIPPING.

DEVILED EGGS, ALWAYS A HIT.

HALVED RADISHES WITH SALT AND BUTTER.

A BIG PLATTER OF PRAWNS WITH COCKTAIL SAUCE.

OYSTERS ON THE HALF SHELL WITH MIGNONETTE SAUCE.

CRAB CAKES WITH REMOULADE SAUCE.

FIGS TOPPED WITH GORGONZOLA.

SAUSAGE ROLLS SERVED WITH A BOWL OF DIJON.

BAKED BRIE WITH CHERRY JAM.

AN EASY ROSÉ TASTING

Having a wine tasting can be as simple as putting out a variety of wines for folks to try. Summer speaks of rosé, so we often have a little tasting out on the island as guests are arriving for Sunday supper. It sparks conversation—how some like it sweeter, others lighter, others more intense. Side conversations are struck up, guests can help themselves to refills, laughter begins. It is a festive way to start a dinner party.

A GLIMPSE OF A COCKTAIL PARTY

Simple, heavy white platters and bowls are go-tos, as they allow the food to be the star.

CITRUS LOVE

When citrus is at its most plentiful and I find bags of it at the grocery store, we like to host a gathering around it. Citrus becomes the theme and all the drinks offered have it as an ingredient. Think gimlets, Harvey Wallbangers, sidecars, and G&Ts. We make the first one for guests and have everything set up in the kitchen so they can help themselves throughout the party. Plus, people love playing with our citrus juicer!

how to: ASSEMBLE A NOSH AND A NIBBLE

We really like to have a good variety of things set out for a nosh with cocktails when guests first arrive. Often, I just set it out on the bar, then move it into the living room once everyone has arrived and we are sitting and chatting before dinner. The point is to enjoy the time with our friends and not be stuck in the kitchen cooking. The best choices are ones that can be bought ahead and stored in the pantry, at the ready for a meal with friends or set out for a party. Here are some suggestions to get you started. Pick and choose.

3 TO 5 CHEESES: BLUE, BRIE, CHEDDAR, CHÈVRE, TRIPLE-CRÈME

VARIETY OF CRACKERS, THINK TALL AND ROUND; MORE VARIETY IS BETTER

SLICED BAGUETTE

JAM OR JAMS

OLIVES AND A SMALL BOWL FOR PITS

MUSTARD OR MUSTARDS

NUTS—CASHEWS, WALNUTS, HAZELNUTS, PISTACHIOS

GRAPES OR FIGS

A BOWL OF CHERRY TOMATOES WITH A SMALL DISH OF SEA SALT NEXT TO IT

SLICED SALAMI

SMOKED SALMON SPREAD

WHITE BEAN DIP

PATÉ, WITH CORNICHONS AND A BIG DOLLOP OF MUSTARD

THE GIFT OF FOOD

NEVER, EVER, EVER UNDERESTI-MATE THE WONDERFULNESS OF THE GIFT OF FOOD. If you are good at making something, make it your signature gift. Our sister-in-law Marian makes the most gloriously beautiful pies. Not only are they works of art to feast your eyes on, but they are also beyond delicious once you cut into them. Hunt for cool vintage receptacles (bowls, platters) to present your gift on or in. That becomes part of the gift that will live on long after the food item has been enjoyed.

CHEESE IS KING

There are times you want to put together a fab appetizer platter, and there are times you want to put together a stellar cheese platter. Depending on the dinner, party, or event, you might even do both. The size of the gathering will dictate that. If your event is large, have platters set at different stations so guests can graze and move about the space with food set all around. It can truly be as easy and simple as a wedge of glorious cheese with fresh figs. Or a platter stuffed to the gills with tons of cheesy options.

A CHEESE PLATTER

Creativity is very helpful when being a good host. It also bumps up the enjoyment factor for you. Cheese platters are one of those things that can make folks instantly turn sweaty. Don't let it do that to you. My best advice is to have the plate or platter full. Only put one type of thing in one place. If you use a grapes, put one bunch out. A mound of figs in another. A whole round of Brie in one spot. A big chunk of Stilton in another. I also like to use individual platters for one type of cheese, and then pair it with something, like jam. Folks love this assortment, as it allows them to try all sorts of combinations they may never have thought of. Like a wedge of triple-crème with a piece of candied ginger. Heaven.

A
STYLISH
GUEST
BATHROOM

While hosting a
party, the guest
bathroom should
be stellar.

A fresh bottle or bar of soap,
plentiful hand towels, extra rolls
of toilet paper. A flowering plant
or blooms, room spray, and a lit,
scented candle.

MANNERS

Being a good host and being a
good guest both come down to good manners.

BE THOUGHTFUL.
BE CHEERFUL.
Both will make the time together
lovely and memorable.

BE HELPFUL.
It is always appreciated.
Even if the help is not needed,
the offer will be remembered.

ASK QUESTIONS.
Most people love a chance to talk
about themselves and their life.

HAVE A STORY TO TELL.
It is always nice to have
an interesting or funny story
to share up your sleeve.

**IF YOU SAY YOU ARE
GOING TO ATTEND, DO SO.**
If you don't feel well, the moment
you wake up in the morning, call to
cancel. Any later is bad form.

TURN OFF YOUR PHONE.
Or at the very least, put it on silent
mode. Being present and in the
moment is key.

**ARRIVE ON TIME AND BE ONE
OF THE FIRST TO DEPART.**
Being late is anything but
fashionable.

OFFER A FIRM HANDSHAKE.
Look someone in the eyes when
they speak, and always listen
attentively.

ALWAYS TALK WITH GUESTS
seated on both sides of you.

WRITE A THANK-YOU NOTE
to your host the day after the event.
Some even like to write it right
when they get home from the
dinner or party.

G&Ts
3 THREE
WAYS

A G&T is be one of the simplest cocktails to make but it can also be one of the most satisfying. Using the very best ingredients is key, as so few make the drink. We like to offer a variety of options to mix it up a bit!

AN AMERICAN G&T

Uncle Val's botanical gin, Jack Rudy Tonic Water, a wedge of lime, ice.

A BRITISH G&T

Hendrick's gin, Fever-Tree tonic water, a cucumber stick, ice.

A FRENCH G&T

Citadelle Gin, Fever-Tree tonic water, a wedge of lemon, ice.

STOOP COCKTAILS

Our entertaining during 2020 was almost nonexistent, other than stoop cocktails with a few close friends. I would make four drinks, almost always a Negroni, and have them on a platter with a large lip so they would not slide off. This was carried to the elevator, and we would be ready to greet our two guests outside of our building in Seattle. They would sit on the bottom steps and we would sit at the top—more than six feet apart from one another. It was a way to connect during an incredibly stressful time. We would all enjoy our cocktails and when we had finished, so was our gathering. We look back on them with great fondness. Mister Sive said to me the other day, "You should totally write about stoop cocktails!" He was right. The concept is rock solid and we are going to continue them long after the pandemic is behind us. We will add hugs and probably not sit so far apart, but meeting friends for a quick drink is such a fun way to stay connected. Often, folks don't want to entertain because of all the work involved. Stoop cocktails could not be easier, and they require as little work as possible in the hosting arena. Cheers to friendship!

An assortment of to-do lists from past gatherings.

I am a big believer in writing things down. It can be such a drag getting home from doing errands for your gathering and realizing you forgot one thing. I have certainly learned my lesson the hard way on this one. Be it for a big grocery shop or a quick run in to pick up a few things, a list can be a lifesaver.

To me, good design is about moments.

Tiny little moments that occur when you walk about a room or a home. Your eye lands on the perfectly faded vessel of field flowers among the flickering candles; your nose picks up the slightest scent of pine from the candle burning somewhere in the room. The crackle of the fire comforts you. A small painting on the wall intrigues and calls you to move closer. The roasted chicken in the oven wafts about. Miles Davis fills the air. The senses are all engaged, and you feel as if you are getting a hug from an old friend. Good design should not be about how much money is spent but about how much care and thought went into a table setting, a room, a home.

POLISHING SILVER

Polishing silver ranks pretty high on my list of activities that help any worries drift away for a bit. Plus, it is hugely satisfying. Our vintage English hotel silver we have collected over the years was looking less than stellar. The other morning after taking Bailey out, I looked at it, shook my head, and headed right for the cabinet where we store the polish. I use Wright's Silver Cream, which is in a small tub. It has a sponge inside that you use to apply the cream. I do it over the sink, then wash the pieces with soap and water when I am done. After drying them off with a cotton towel, they all look like new. As I have already said, the process is crazy satisfying. We use the silver in some way almost every day, so we leave it all out at the ready. That way we can enjoy it visually when not in use and can easily reach for it when a piece is called into action. Using silver in your day-to-day is such a simple luxury. I don't know about you—but my guess is that we are on the same page with this one—I cling to all the little things that bring me happiness and joy in a very big way during unsettling times. Simple things or routines can add so much to our day, and ultimately our lives.

"Instructions for living a life: Pay attention. Be astonished. Tell about it." —Mary Oliver

READY FOR A PARTY!

PUTTING TOGETHER A PARTY CAN BE QUITE A BIT OF WORK.
Okay, lots of work! Once the day arrives, take a deep breath. Continue this throughout the day. You have your lists. You are checking things off as you go. You've got this. The hour or half hour before guests are due to arrive, walk around the party space, whether it's a room or rooms. Wherever guests will be. Scan as you go. Fix flowers, light candles, check the ice buckets. Now is the time to have a quick chat with those who are helping you, be it one or many. All the tiny pieces that join to make a memorable gathering, now is the time to tend to them. Once that first guest arrives, you want all these little details complete. Remember, you are going to have one swell time at your own party, and you are not going to worry or fret once it has begun.

DEARLY BELOVED,
WE ARE GATHERED HERE TODAY
TO GET THROUGH THIS THING
CALLED LIFE.

—PRINCE

GIFTS TO GIVE AS GUESTS DEPART

A CELLO BAG WITH A BOTTLE OF PERRIER, A VELLUM ENVELOPE WITH TWO ASPIRINS, AND A FEW WRAPPED CARAMELS OR CHOCOLATES. THIS IS ALWAYS A HIT ON THE RIDE HOME.

A POMANDER YOU MADE. POMANDERS BRING BACK SUCH FOND MEMORIES OF CHILDHOOD.

TINS OF LOUIS SHERRY TRUFFLES. THE ICONIC TIN BECOMES A KEEPSAKE.

SMALL BOX OF JONBOY SALTED CARAMELS.

SMALL LITTLE BOOK ON FRIENDSHIP THAT YOU HAVE INSCRIBED BEFOREHAND.

CUPCAKE IN A TRAVEL CONTAINER, ALONG WITH A PAPER NAPKIN.

BAG OF HOMEMADE GRANOLA FOR BREAKFAST THE NEXT MORNING.

BUNDLE OF BLOOMS FROM YOUR GARDEN IN A CLEAR GLASS WECK JAR.

HANDWRITTEN RECIPE CARD ATTACHED TO A SMALL BOX WITH THE INGREDIENTS TO MAKE YOUR FAVOR-ITE COCKTAIL, DIP, OR SWEET TREAT.

A SMALL SCENTED CANDLE AND A BATH FIZZ FOR A SOAK WHEN THEY GET HOME.

SMALL CELLO BAG OF COFFEE BEANS SO COFFEE IS ON YOU THE NEXT MORNING.

A STYLISH CANDY CUBE OF SUGARFINA WATER-MELON SLICES FOR THE RIDE HOME.

AN INSPIRED QUOTE YOU HAVE HANDWRITTEN ON A TAG THAT IS HANGING OFF THOUGHTFULLY PACKAGED LEFT-OVERS. CHINESE TAKEOUT BOXES WORK GRAND FOR THIS.

YOUR FAVORITE SINGLE BLOOM IN A WATER TUBE SO YOU AND YOUR EVENT WILL BE SWEETLY REMEMBERED FOR THE WEEK AHEAD.

BEST PARTY

I asked my blog readers, "What is your best party memory?"

We live in the country. My best party memory is in the blink of an eye, our country lane filling with vehicles. Our family, friends and neighbors had arrived!

Dancing in the living room after the rugs are rolled up and the veranda doors are wide open. Disco lights, fog machine, and endless glasses of Champagne.

Our neighbor had a black-tie dinner at their house. Bentley, our English Sheepdog, ran through their muddy lawn, and as the man opened the door to greet his guests, Bentley jumped up onto the shoulders of his tuxedo!

At 60, I threw myself a catered party in my home with all my closest friends. Dining tables placed in every room! At each place setting I had a special photo of each friend from sometime in the past. It was magical. Bailey, our French Bulldog, wore a bow tie.

Oysters, Champagne, the ocean, and my beloved.

It was a small dinner party 20 years ago . . . three couples. After dinner, we had dessert outside by the fireplace where three guitars were set up. The three husbands spontaneously serenaded us. Such a great memory!

My Southern grandmother serving cucumber sandwiches on her oval glass plates with matching punch cups that fit perfectly on the plate.

As kids, NYE celebrations with our neighbors, throwing streamers and confetti to the adults below as they wore hats and fancy clothes, hugging and cheek-kissing.

When my friend threw me a surprise 50th birthday party! Imagine everyone you love in a small, intimate setting. Magical!

While celebrating my husband at his 50th, I looked around and could see our favorite people, hear their chatter and laughing, see them drinking and eating, and it filled my cup.

MEMORIES

My daughter and I were flying to Paris for my 60th birthday. We flew business class. Our meal began with Champagne and foie gras. I didn't want the flight to end!

Meeting my future husband at a party for a mutual friend's college graduation. That relationship didn't last, but ours has. We're celebrating 27 years of marriage in September.

Each Christmas, our empty-nester neighbors would throw a party for the entire block. They would decorate a tree in each room, dress up as Mr. and Mrs. Claus, and pass out a wrapped gift to every single child. The parties are a kaleidoscope of memories for me: music, red velvet dresses and bows, poinsettia by the fireplace, homemade butter mints on every side table.

My best friend's amazing wedding over thirty years ago in an English country house. Elegant, relaxed, and charming. Pink Champagne, delicious, exquisite canapés, candles everywhere, glowing firelight, the scent of a beautiful fall day and a lounge pianist completing the most perfect celebration.

For my 40th surprise birthday party, my husband asked guests to each bring a rose bush for a gift. Then in the following weeks he built a beautiful rose garden for me!

Approaching a cocktail party in heavy fog to the tune of a saxophone. As we reached the porch, the saxophonist was leaning under a gaslight by the door playing his heart out.

My dear friend was recently married and came to visit with her partner. We had an intimate dinner and then followed dessert with a surprise game of blind man's buff in the solarium. There was so much laughter, we felt like kids again.

Whether it is a 5-star meal with elegant decor and clothes, or a casual meal around the grill, or an impromptu drop-in where a meal just comes together when taking everything out of the fridge-- my memory of great parties always has the smiles and laughter of friends brought together around food. The sharing of food makes my heart sing!

My daughter's wedding in a B&B in Bedford, NY. All the important people in my life in one place at one time. It can never be repeated.

WHAT IS YOUR BEST PARTY MEMORY?

FLOWER POWER

BEAUTIMOUS BLOOMS

If you leaf through this book, you'll instantly see that flowers hold a very special place in my heart. I like giving them, receiving them, and using them at home and in the shops any chance I get. Flowers can be expensive, so I try and be super smart about buying them.

Buy in season. The best deal on tulips is in the spring, when they are most plentiful. If a friend has a big garden, always let them know you would be happy to take any excess off their hands. Many of our friends have big yards with glorious gardens, and they often bring me flowers when their gardens are overflowing. Grocery stores almost always have an assortment of flowers that can often be purchased for a good deal. If you have a yard, plant bulbs and flowering plants that you can cut and use inside. Be it a vase with one beautimous bloom or an ice bucket overflowing with stems, flowers make your home, gathering, or party memorable and special beyond measure.

CHOOSING FLOWERS

Ahhhh, flowers. I can't imagine being a host without them. The happiness they give me is certainly destined to transfer to our guests. Flowers, for many, can be intimidating. My goal here is to show it not.

CHOOSE ONE TYPE OF FLOWER. This is often my approach. Use what is in season. Much like produce, seasonal flowers will be freshest and will most certainly be the best deal. I generally choose one color, and then run with it. Placing flowers on side tables, in the bathroom, on the dining table. Several bunches picked up at the farmers market, grocery store, corner bodega, or clipped from your garden will do the trick and be awesome.

GO LOW. Flowers on the dining table are always best kept short so guests can easily see over them. You don't want folks staring right into the flowers at eye level. Unscented or lightly scented is best. I would never use lilies or other heavily fragranced flowers on a dining table. You want the delicious scent of your food to take center stage.

STICK WITH ONE COLOR. One color allows the grouping to be a cohesive whole. A big bundle of monochromatic dahlias or tulips arranged together can look as if they were plucked from the garden. Flower arranging can be intimidating. This method helps take away some of the guesswork.

SPREAD ABOUT SINGLE-STEM VASES. Where would I be without single-stem vases? They are the backbone of my flower arranging, allowing a single bloom to shine its utmost. A lone, glorious lily on a side table or the bathroom sink is sure to be admired. (Plus, this is where their divine scent will be absolutely appreciated.) I often run single-stem vases down the middle of the dining table to create an orderly little garden amongst the dinnerware. It really could not be easier. What can you use for a single-stem vase? Drinking glasses, vintage bottles. Scale is key. You don't want the bloom to be overpowered by the vessel. In turn, you don't want the single-stem vase to be dominated by the flower. Trust your eye. You will know.

ASK A FLOWERY FRIEND. If you know someone who has a killer garden, ask if they would cut some flowers for you. So often they will be delighted. We don't have outside space at our apartment in town, so I often ask friends who have big yards or gardens if they would cut some things for me. It is kind of like sharing baked goods. Those who have access to it are generally thrilled to share.

WHEN IN DOUBT, ASK A PROFESSIONAL. There are so many super-talented floral folks out there. Many have shops; others work on their own doing special events. Their expertise can lead to stunning arrangements, and mean flowers are one thing you can cross off your party to-do list.

IN LOVE WITH HERBS

Using herbs in place of flowers or mixed in with them has been a favorite trick of mine for as long as I can remember. A fun memory is being at our friend Cara's house in Southold, on the North Fork of Long Island, during a crazy humid and hot August—which we adore in a big way. It means summmmaaaaaa to both of us! The zinnias at the farmers market looked divine. I bought a big mixed bunch. Cara had a rosemary bush in her yard that seemed like it was on steroids. It was gloriously huge. I snipped a bunch of stems and added them to the zinnia arrangements I had put together in old silver pitchers and dotted around her house. It was a simple gift, one we knew she would enjoy long after we said our goodbyes and headed back to the city. The scent and the "green" of the rosemary paired with all the vibrant-colored zinnias was such a happy combo.

When herbs are plentiful in
the warm months, running herb
bouquets down the middle of
the dining table is one of my
go-to, easy table settings. Our
pots of herbs grow like weeds
out at WestWard when they bake
in the sun all day. **SNIP,
SNIP, AND WE ARE ALL
SET TO ENJOY SUPPER**
surrounded by the bounty.

FOR THE LOVE
OF FLOWERS

Usually the number one item on my hosting list, even before the food or drink, are the flowers. Fresh flowers or flowering plants add a touch to a room or a table that can create lasting memories. After leaving a sublime party or dinner, what I often remember most is the flowers. Done well, they add a flourish that can be truly unforgettable. At this point, you know I don't think this must break the bank—just go out your front door and pluck some stems. **CREATIVITY IN YOUR FLORAL DECISIONS IS KEY.** A table filled with potted geraniums that you can later plant outside is heaven. A scattered row of vintage bottles holding long stems of French tulips, picked up at the grocery store, is a sight to behold. An orchid on the sink in the guest bathroom to be enjoyed while folks wash their hands. A crystal ice bucket brimming with peonies on a coffee table might never be forgotten. Think of flowers much like you would your jewelry. Like a great pair of earrings or a necklace, flowers are an accent that can pull your entire room or table together.

To me, flowers go hand in hand with hosting. **FLOWERS EVOKE GRACIOUSNESS.** Whether big bunches or little single stem vases dotted about, either or both are always appropriate. They just bring happiness, plain and simple. Here are my thoughts on blooms:

- **LIKE PRODUCE, BUY IN SEASON.** You'll get the freshest, best quality. You are also going to get the best deal then too.

- **THINK OUTSIDE THE BOX.** Ask friends who have gardens. Walk a country road and pluck as you go. There are plenty of ways to have your home or table overflowing with blooms without spending a dime.

- **STAY WITH ONE COLOR STORY.** Easy on the eyes and easy to make arrangements.

- **STAY WITH ONE TYPE OF FLOWER.** Same as above.

- **CONSIDER SCENT.** I tend to stay away from scented flowers on the dinner table and place them around the house instead.

- **BIG VERSUS SMALL.** Use big arrangements where you can stand back and enjoy them and small ones on side tables and bathrooms.

- **USE POTTED PLANTS.** Plants from garden centers are a great way to add blooms to your settings without breaking a sweat. Always put them in a stylish-looking pot, planter, or container.

- **THINK OUTSIDE THE BOX.** If flowers are not inspiring you, use branches, bowls of fruit, or even produce. Vases of asparagus are a personal favorite.

THE JOY OF PAPER FLOWERS

I must admit, I am not a big fan of faux flowers. Not that I have anything against them; it is just that my love of fresh flowers and plants runs so deep. But then I met paper flowers. Wow. A game changer for me. More like a piece of art, they are not trying to "be" real flowers; they are trying to be themselves. You can see that they are paper, but done well, they absolutely sing. That is where artist Livia Cetti comes in. We have been carrying her work at Watson Kennedy for a good number of years. My first introduction to her floral creations was at John Derian's shop in New York. We have carried John's decoupage works at WK for over twenty years, and I have been going to his shop (now shops) for as long. They are a must anytime we are in the city.

When we bought our house, Hawthorne, in the Hudson Valley, I knew one of our first purchases would be a Livia Cetti geranium plant, which I had long coveted. Our first trip into the city after taking possession of the house, I marched right in, eying the paper geranium in the photo. It sat on my lap on the drive all the way back up the Taconic Parkway. We now have several at the house, as they are perfect when we are away. **NO WATERING REQUIRED!** We also have the single stems lining the upper shutters at our Seattle home, like they are growing out of the windows. They make for creative table settings too. Guests are completely taken with them, gazing upon the floral works of art as we dine away.

THE POWER OF PINK

Pink blooms instantly make a table or room pretty, be it a big bundle of peonies, tulips, or dahlias, or even a tall, scented geranium topiary with the sweetest pink blooms. **THE HUE PACKS A HAPPY VISUAL PUNCH.**

THE MAGIC OF GERANIUMS

The beauty of potted geraniums is that they can easily be called into action when you are setting a table, either inside or out. Slip them into a cachepot or leave them just as they are in their terra-cotta pots. **YOU INSTANTLY GET A VIBRANT HIT OF GREEN.** Even when not flowering, they still have the loveliest vibe going on. And when they begin to flower, the blooms are the icing on the cake.

"Anyone who keeps the ability to see beauty never grows old."
—Franz Kafka

TKW

TED'S TIP
№ 13

Use vintage or new
plates that work with
the table setting
as the saucers for
potted plants. It is
a small detail with
big visual impact.

Farm stands and farmers markets are great places to find flowers that you don't often see or find other places. Campanula, or Canterbury bells, were the inspiration for this creamy white zen table. **SIMPLICITY WAS THE THEME,** vintage apothecary bottles as the single-stem vessels were called into action. A chilled soup and grilled fish on the menu.

KALE
IN A PINCH

Kale is often so plentiful at the farmers market, farm stands, and the grocery store that I reach for it time and again when the flowers being offered are not inspiring me. It gives an instant hit of green, and guests always comment on the cleverness of the arrangements. Plus, I love that it does double duty, as a big salad can be made with it the next day for lunch or dinner. Kale is indeed a superfood as well as a super go-to in a pinch.

TED'S TIP
No. 14

Use the leaves of
flowers, in this case
hydrangeas, as place
cards. It is an earthy,
use-what-you-have,
resourceful way
to be creative. Use
markers or crayons
or watercolors to
write the names.

HYDRANGEAS AT ERIKA'S

Not having a yard in town means I count on the kindness of our friends to
supply us with beautiful blooms when their plants are overflowing. We are
always happy recipients! Our friend Erika shares these lovelies from her
garden with us throughout the season. These speak to me of summer in
every way. A tight bundle or an overflowing bouquet, either is incredibly
visual and satisfying to the eye and soul.

A ZEST FOR ZINNIAS

Normally, herbs like rosemary are my go-to with zinnias, but the carrot top greens were looking so pretty from the bunch we picked up at the Hudson Farmers Market, I decided to give them a go. **ALWAYS BE THINKING OUTSIDE THE BOX** when looking for, buying, or assembling flowers.

TO SIP

A HStartY MEMORY

While I was growing up, my parents always traveled with an incredibly stylish piece of luggage that actually housed a mini bar. My folks were mighty popular with the other parents from my junior tennis circuit. They knew cocktails would be happening at 5 o'clock where the Watsons were set up watching matches. Just typing that makes me happy—it is such a fun memory of my parents and how they could always make it a party, no matter where they were. I have followed in their footsteps, as my husband and I love to host a party whenever we can. Here are a few of my favorite libations, both to serve guests and to drink myself.

A WESTWARD MARTINI

MAKES 1 DRINK

Sitting by the fire reading a book is a lovely thing. But sitting by the fire reading a book while sipping on a martini is a really lovely thing. I think of martinis as very social cocktails. A proper martini glass, laughter, friends. But I have been enjoying an abbreviated version before dinner on the week- end. A WestWard martini is my quick version of a favorite cocktail that avoids all of the bells and whistles.

Ice cube	**1 or 2 pitted**
1 shot cold gin	**green olives**
Dash of vermouth	

A simple glass will do. Shake gin with a dash of vermouth if you must, but pouring it right into the glass is fine too. If the bottle of gin has been in the freezer, all the better. The key is having a large ice cube in the glass, waiting. I have been into jumbo ice cubes of late. Skewer an olive or two and you are set. **BOOK OPTIONAL.**

A MARTINI, MY WAY

MAKES 2 DRINKS

If it is Friday evening, it is pretty close to a sure bet that I will be having a martini and Mister Sive will be having a Gibson. Both of those cocktails will be made with gin. Always. I am the mixologist in the family, so it will be me making them. I am of the shaken, not stirred family. Because of my love of ice, I like my martini realllly cold.

Several shots cold gin
¼ capful of vermouth

Skewered olive stuffed
with a garlic clove

Fill shaker to the top with ice. Then pour in your favorite gin. We are big Hendrick's fans. This is a very grown-up cocktail, by the way. We never drive after having one of these, and guests most always cab to our home if they are invited. I like to keep the gin in the freezer so it is icy cold right out of the gate. The gin does not have to be this way, but the drink is especially great if it is. Next, vermouth. I like vermouth, but I don't want it to overpower the drink, which it can. I use a quarter of a capful, from the bottle. Then shake that shaker vigorously. I think of it as my Friday eve exercise. Pour the drink into a martini glass that has skewered olives awaiting. A friend got me hooked on olives stuffed with a garlic clove, which are quite dandy. Any good-quality olive will do; just make sure there is no pit involved. Sit, relax, enjoy.

A PHONE-TINI

Being a retailer during the holidays means little to no travel since being away from the shops is just not in the picture. But I still long to see close friends who live far away to catch up on what is happening in their lives and just have a nice, long chat. That is where the phone-tini comes in. Sitting and chatting with a friend whilst having a cocktail rates pretty high in my book. The phone-tini allows that to happen during a long-distance call. It is absolutely best if both parties are enjoying a phone-tini at the same time. A perfect way to end a busy, busy day.

A REVERSE MARTINI

MAKES 1 DRINK

I am the type of martini drinker who often does not even open the vermouth while making my own. Just glancing at the bottle while I am shaking the shaker away is just fine by me. So the fact that I like a reverse martini comes as quite a big surprise. This all came about when I was finishing up my read of Dearie, *about Julia Child. Whether or not she came up with this idea I am uncertain, but it was the first I had ever heard of it.*

A reverse martini is $^2/_3$ vermouth to $^1/_3$ gin, shaken, and then served over ice. I first gave this a try at Hawthorne and really liked it. Extremely refreshing. It has the feel of a summer drink. I don't usually drink martinis during the hot months since they get warm instead of staying super chilled, which is how I really like them. Plus, a big tub of gin in the heat makes me sleepy. With the reverse martini, **THE VERMOUTH BECOMES THE STAR.** *The gin is just a stylish background singer. A fresh bottle of vermouth is helpful. My study on the topic found that vermouth can lose a bit of its fabulousness when old. So often a bottle can last ages, so it's easy to see this happening. We had a newish bottle of Dolin that worked quite lovely. Julia preferred Noilly Prat, so we picked up a bottle. I think I actually preferred the Noilly. Julia got it right again.*

Ice   1 shot gin

2 shots vermouth

Place ice in a martini glass. Pour vermouth and gin into a shaker and shake. Pour over ice. Enjoy.

A FRENCH 75

MAKES 1 DRINK

We would have French 75s over the years, but close to the date of my fiftieth birthday party, we had some after a long absence, and I fell in love with the drink all over again. So much so that it became the signature cocktail of my B-day bash. What is not to love when you mix two of my favorites, Veuve Clicquot Champagne with Hendrick's gin? I also adore Meyer lemons, so they got a nice twist of that too. But, really, any type of bubbly and gin will do. Oh my. They indeed pack a punch, as many of our guests can attest. In a beautiful flute, a French 75 is **JUST ABOUT AS FESTIVE AND CELEBRATORY AS A DRINK CAN BE.** *Be sure to have a rideshare app on your phone if you drink more than one!*

1 shot gin   **Twist of lemon**
Chilled Champagne to fill flute

Pour shot of gin in flute. Top with Champagne. Add twist of lemon.

Always have nonalcoholic drink options on hand. We are big fans of San Pellegrino Italian sodas. Ginger ale, 7UP, club soda, and sparkling water are great basics that every good home bar should have at the ready.

Hearty nibbles are key when serving cocktails. It is important to offer guests a bit of food in addition to a drink.

A WINE TASTING

Having a wine tasting can be as simple as putting out a big bucket of the same type of wine after it has just been released. **IT IS A FESTIVE WAY TO BEGIN A DINNER PARTY.** Guests can pour a glass and take a walk on the beach or settle into a favorite chair. It is a great way to try new wines or a tried-and-true favorite. One of mine is Domaine Tempier Bandol Rosé, which holds a special place in my heart.

TED'S TIP
NO. 17

Snacking Tomatoes: This is a summer entertaining staple in our house when tomatoes are plentiful and at their best. Rinse off cherry tomatoes and put into a lovely bowl. Some of the water can stay on them, which you want, as it helps them grab the salt. Fill another lovely bowl or saucer (vintage saucers make great food-holding vessels) with chunky sea salt. We are big fans of Maldon or Jacobsen. I also like to put a big dollop of the salt right on the board next to the tomatoes. Guests dip the tomato into the salt. It is a fantastic accompaniment to a variety of other tasty treats, as the tomatoes are nice and light. Even healthy!

A NEGRONI

MAKES 1 DRINK

This is a drink that I enjoyed in my showroom days, sort of forgot about it, was served a few years ago by friends in the Berkshires, and have fully embraced once again. Italian in origin, it is an aperitif, meaning something you enjoy before a meal. It packs a punch, so for me it is always just one. During an outdoor shower at WestWard before I start putting supper together is one of my favorite ways to enjoy a Negroni. It is also quite fun to make a big tray of them for when folks first arrive to a dinner party.

Ice	Shot of Campari
Shot of gin	1 orange slice
Shot of vermouth rosso	

In a rocks glass or tumbler, add a good amount of ice. Then pour a shot of gin, a shot of vermouth rosso, and a shot of Campari. These should all be in equal parts. The color combination is quite something. Lastly, twist an orange slice over the concoction and add said slice to the drink. Stir. Be happy. Outdoor shower optional.

TED'S TIP
NO. 18

For a quick appetizer to serve with drinks, smash (either with a fork or food processor) cooked peas along with some mint, EVOO and salt and pepper. Set atop a toasted baguette slice that is slathered with ricotta laced with lemon zest.

MY BLOODY MARY

MAKES 1 DRINK

Ice cubes

2 shots vodka

1 (11.5-ounce) can V8

Sea salt and freshly ground
   black pepper, to taste

2 shakes Worcestershire sauce

3 drops Tabasco sauce

Wedge of lime

1 spear pickled asparagus, plus
   1 spoonful of the juice

Get your favorite good-size glass and fill it halfway with ice. Pour in 2 shots of your favorite vodka. I am an Absolut fan, as was my dad, so this is also in remembrance of him. Add as much of a can of V8 as your glass will hold, preferably an entire can. Add a few pinches of sea salt and a few cracks of freshly ground pepper. Then add 2 shakes of Worcestershire sauce and 3 drops of Tabasco sauce. Squeeze the lime into the glass and add the wedge to the cocktail. I am not a big fan of celery, and I also think it takes up precious room for vodka, so I like to add a pickled asparagus spear. Lastly, I add a spoonful of the pickling juice (which is vinegar and garlic) that the asparagus has been sitting in. I find this last step adds an amazing extra depth of flavor to the Bloody Mary. Stir and enjoy.

TO TASTE

BREAKING BREAD
WITH THOSE YOU LOVE

Breaking bread with those you love can mean many different things to each of us, and there are many different ways in which to celebrate together. The unifying element, though, is food. Sharing a meal you have cooked or assembled is an act of love. Be it a simple something or a grand feast, the important thing is that you are doing it. Here are some of my favorite things to make when we have a small gathering or a crowd.

"If you can't feed one hundred people, then feed just one." —Mother Teresa

CHICKEN WITH MEYER LEMONS, OLIVES & ROSEMARY

This easy Provençal-inspired dish feels a bit like summer, even when it is not. I prefer thighs to white meat for this, as they stay moist. I prefer skinless, as it produces way less fat, and the sauce at the end becomes part of the dish. If you are not a dark meat fan, then for sure try it with breast meat; just watch super carefully to not overcook the meat.

4 skinless boneless chicken thighs
Extra-virgin olive oil
Salt
Pepper
Few sprigs fresh rosemary
Handful of pitted olives

3 Meyer lemons
White wine
Basmati or jasmine rice, or egg noodles, for serving

Heat oven to 400°F.

Place skinless boneless chicken thighs in a baking dish. Add olive oil and season with salt and pepper. Then add a few sprigs of rosemary and a handful of olives. Cut up Meyer lemons, some in half and some in quarters, and tuck them here and there among the chicken. Lastly, pour over a bit of good white wine to moisten the entire mixture. Roast in the oven for 45 minutes, or until the chicken registers 165°F on a thermometer. Several times during the cooking process, move things around a bit in the dish. Start spooning the juice that is being created over the meat. Add more white wine if you think more liquid is needed.

End result, you will get super-moist chicken along with an amazing sauce that the lemons, olives, rosemary, olive oil, and chicken drippings have produced. Serve over basmati or jasmine rice or egg noodles, being sure to ladle over that precious sauce. The Meyer lemons are edible, skin and all, so give those a try too. This is easy enough for a weeknight meal but also has an earthy quality that makes it a stellar meal to serve guests.

ZUCCHINI & POTATO TIAN

A tian is such a lovely dish to make for nestling next to fish or a piece of chicken. It can stand alone as a vegetarian offering as well. I like how it includes potatoes and a veg, which make it super hearty. Adding the cheese takes it over the top, in a very good way. Your kitchen will smell heavenly. When shopping for ingredients, you'll want to choose Yukon Gold potatoes and zucchini that are very similar in circumference so things cook evenly.

Extra virgin olive oil	**3 to 4 medium-**
1 sweet onion	**size zucchini**
3 cloves garlic,	**Salt**
finely minced	**Pepper**
6 to 8 stems fresh	**5 to 8 ounces**
thyme, divided	**Gruyère cheese,**
1 pound medium-size	**shredded**
Yukon Gold potatoes	

Heat oven to 375°F while you get things chopping.

Cut up one sweet onion. In a skillet over medium heat, add 2 tablespoons of olive oil and let it heat up. Add your chopped onion and cook until it turns translucent. Add the minced garlic before the onions are done and cook for just a few minutes. Be careful not to overcook the garlic, as it becomes bitter fast. You want it sweet. Line the bottom of a baking dish with the sautéed onions and garlic. Pull thyme leaves off half the stems and sprinkle all around the onion-garlic mixture. This is the base. It is fine that this cools while you're chopping away.

Cut potatoes and zucchini into 1/4-inch rounds. On top of the onions, start stacking rows of the slices in the baking dish, alternating as you go—zucchini, potato, zucchini, potato. They should be leaning on one another. Once done, add a light sprinkle of extra virgin olive oil and liberal sprinkling of salt over the top of things. A bit of pepper too. Add more thyme leaves over the lot as well. The herb is so mellow and really adds to the lusciousness of this dish. Finally, add a few whole springs of the thyme to the dish, cover with aluminum foil and bake for 45 minutes.

Take the casserole out of oven, remove the foil and the whole thyme stems and discard. Add a generous—make that a super-generous—amount of shredded Gruyère cheese to the entire top of the dish. Take extra care to make sure the cheese has also fallen down the sides of the mixture. You really want all of this cheesy goodness spread everywhere once it is melted. Place casserole back into the oven, uncovered, for another 30 minutes to finish cooking and to melt the cheese. Trust me, you will be quite pleased with yourself. It is so darn good! The cooked and melted mixture of the onions and garlic with the potatoes and zucchini, all mixed with the herbaceous goodness of the thyme, is really quite something.

DUNGENESS CRAB, CORN & WHITE CHEDDAR FRITTATA

Here is the general method I use when making the frittata. It absolutely can be made smaller or larger by adjusting the number of eggs and volume of added ingredients. Prep and cut the precooked seafood, meat, and vegetables into bite-size pieces. Shred the cheese. All should be ready before the eggs hit the heat.

5 eggs
Milk
Pinch of salt
Pinch of pepper
1 to 2 tablespoons butter

Dungeness crab pieces, precooked
$1/2$ cup fresh corn off the cob
1 cup shredded white
  cheddar cheese

Turn the broiler on high to get it heated. Heat a skillet with an ovenproof handle over low heat.

Break 5 eggs into a bowl. (I generally do 2 eggs per person and add an extra at the end just to make sure it is hearty). Whisk eggs with a splash of milk and pinches of salt and pepper.

Over very low heat, add a knob of butter to the skillet and melt it, making sure it covers the entire surface of the pan, including the walls. This assures the eggs do not stick when they puff up in the oven. Add the beaten egg mixture to the pan. Since it is on low heat, it will take a bit of time for the eggs to start to set. They will still be quite liquid in the middle, but the sides will start to firm up. At this point, add your fillings.

Add the cooked crab and corn and then the white cheddar cheese. Cook that a bit as the egg mixture firms up even more. You will not cook it completely on the stove top; the center will cook in the oven. Once the sides are firm and the whole thing seems to be setting a bit, it is now ready to go under the broiler. This is when the magic happens. I stay with it the entire time, as this can go quickly. Make sure you're wearing an ovenproof mitt since the pan handle will get crazy hot. Speaking from past experience. (Insert smile here.) This beautiful thing will puff up and start to get a bit golden brown in spots. Move the pan around to make sure it is cooking evenly. It will continue to puff up—my favorite part—until the center is cooked through, which you will be able to determine by sight. You can also take it out and press your finger on the middle. It should have a little give but be firm. Done! Slice up and enjoy. We like this for breakfast, brunch, lunch, dinner. A big salad nestled up to it is grand. Enjoy.

Some other favorite frittata combinations:

Black Forest Ham & Cheddar

Herbed Chèvre & Fresh Corn

Parmigiano-Reggiano & Roasted Cauliflower

Smoked Salmon & Chèvre

Mushroom Mélange & Beecher's Flagship Cheese

Parmesan & Mushroom

PARMESAN SMASHED POTATOES

When you have leftover baby Yukon gold potatoes and want to make them a little extra special the next go-round, smash them then load them up with Parmesan cheese.

Leftover baked Yukon
   Gold potatoes*
Extra-virgin olive oil
Salt
Pepper
Freshly grated
   Parmesan cheese

First, take a fork, gently push down on the spud until it flattens out a bit. Then sprinkle all about with freshly grated Parmesan. Either microwave to reheat or put in the oven at 350°F to warm and crisp up. Super easy, super yummy. You'd never know they are leftovers.

*If you don't have cooked potatoes, preheat the oven to 400°F and put raw potatoes on a baking sheet. Coat them with extra virgin olive oil; sprinkle with salt and pepper. Bake until soft and ready to smash. Then proceed with the recipe.

MY BASIC VINAIGRETTE

This is the easiest, simplest vinaigrette just as it is, but you can build upon it to create all sorts of others by adding mustard, herbs, shallots, jam, etc.

$1/4$ cup fresh-squeezed lemon juice or white wine vinegar or balsamic vinegar	Salt Pepper $1/2$ cup extra-virgin olive oil

In a measuring cup, add $1/4$ cup of fresh squeezed lemon juice, white wine vinegar, or balsamic vinegar, plus generous pinches of salt and pepper. Then whisk in $1/2$ cup of the best extra-virgin olive oil you can get your hands on.

VEUVE CLICQUOT VINAIGRETTE

Little jars of Veuve Clicquot vinaigrette make great parting gifts after a swell eve. Collect any Champagne remaining at the bottoms of bottles and save it in the fridge, uncorked, for a few days or even weeks. Then turn that liquid gold into a tasty vinaigrette to have on a healthy salad. It is a fun memory from the bottle of Champagne enjoyed earlier.

3 tablespoons Champagne	$1/2$ teaspoon kosher salt
1 tablespoon finely chopped shallots	$1/4$ teaspoon freshly ground pepper
1 teaspoon honey	$1/4$ cup extra-virgin olive oil
1 teaspoon rice wine vinegar	
1 tablespoon Dijon mustard	

Whisk ingredients together until emulsified.

Here are some favorite variations:

Shallot Vinaigrette

Parmesan, Lemon & Mustard Vinaigrette

Really Amazing Herby Vinaigrette

Maple Syrup Vinaigrette

Blood Orange Vinaigrette

Garlic Vinaigrette

CORN DUTCH BABY

An 8- to 12-inch black cast-iron skillet works best, but I have also made this recipe in a nonstick pan and it worked swell.

1/2 cup all-purpose flour	1/8 teaspoon salt
1/2 cup whole milk	3 tablespoons unsalted butter
2 eggs	1 cup freshly cooked
2 tablespoons sugar	corn off the cob

Preheat the oven to 425°F while you mix up the batter.

In a good-size bowl, add 1/2 cup flour, 1/2 cup whole milk, 2 eggs, 2 tablespoons sugar, and 1/8 teaspoon salt. Mix all together. Don't worry if it's a tad lumpy. Set aside.

In a small pan, add a tablespoon of butter and sauté the cup of corn off the cob. Set aside.

On the stovetop, heat your skillet over medium high heat. Add the remaining 2 tablespoons of unsalted butter and let melt, being sure to completely cover the bottom and sides of the skillet.

Add the batter to the skillet. Working quickly, scatter the freshly sautéed corn to the mixture Move the skillet to the oven for 15 to 20 minutes. Check at 15 minuets to see if the pancake has inflated and the edges have browned; if not, cook a bit longer. This is the prettiest, puffiest darn thing right when it comes out of the oven (which makes it soufflé-like), but it will deflate quickly (which makes it pancake-like) and still look yummy. Cut in half or quarters and serve immediately.

CHICKEN BREAST WITH CRACKED PEPPER CHÈVRE

Bone-in, skin-on chicken breast is best for this recipe. The bone really helps to keep the meat moist, and I just like the earthiness of the bone as part of this dish.

2 bone-in, skin-on chicken breasts	Salt
4 ounces plain chèvre	Pepper
Freshly cracked black pepper	
Extra-virgin olive oil	

Preheat the oven to 400°F.

Place the chicken breasts on a work surface and pat dry. Take the chèvre and add a good amount of freshly cracked black pepper to it. Working carefully, slip your finger under the chicken skin and create a pocket. Insert the peppered chèvre into that pocket.

Place the chicken in an ovenproof skillet. Lather chicken breasts with a healthy amount of extra-virgin olive oil. Salt and pepper liberally. Move the skillet to the oven. Depending on the thickness of the breasts, it will take 35 to 45 minutes to cook, until the chicken registers 165°F.

Once done, carefully place the chicken breasts on a platter or plate and cover with aluminum foil to rest for 10 minutes before serving. Then place the beautifully cooked breasts on individual plates and serve whole, one per person.

CAULIFLOWER STEAKS WITH CAPERS, OLIVES & LEMONS

1 head cauliflower

³/₄ cup pitted green olives

Extra-virgin olive oil

2 tablespoons capers

1 lemon, quartered

Salt

Pepper

Preheat oven to 400°F. Lightly oil a rimmed baking sheet.

Make cauliflower steaks by cutting ³/₄-inch-thick slices from the center of the head. Break remaining cauliflower into florets.

I like to lay the two steaks in the middle of the baking sheet and scatter the florets all around. Add olives and capers. Drizzle generously with extra-virgin olive oil. Squeeze the lemon juice over everything. Add spent lemons to the baking sheet. Salt and pepper the lot. Roast for 15 minutes, then turn all and cook another 15 minutes, checking along the way.

ASPARAGUS & GRUYÈRE TART

Use a puff pastry sheet you find in the freezer section at the grocery store. Pepperidge Farm makes my favorite, and we always have a few on hand in the freezer.

1 sheet frozen puff pastry, thawed
Extra-virgin olive oil
2 bundles fresh, thin asparagus,
   ends trimmed

Salt
Pepper
Gruyère cheese

Preheat the oven to 400°F. Thaw one sheet of frozen puff pastry (directions on box) on a parchment-lined baking sheet. Using a sharp knife, create a 1-inch border around the entire piece, making sure not to cut all the way through the pastry. Then take a fork and prick holes inside of the border. Bake for 15 minutes in then remove from oven.

Brush the entire pastry with extra-virgin olive oil. Then lay the asparagus within the border. Salt and pepper liberally. Large grate a good amount of Gruyère directly over all of the asparagus. A heavy hand with the cheese will make you happy later, trust me. Return to the oven for another 20 minutes, until the crust is golden brown and the cheese has melted.

CITRUS BAKED BRIE

Frozen puff pastry is needed. There are usually two sheets in a package you will need just one for this recipe. Pepperidge Farm is the brand I typically find at our grocer, but any is fine. Follow the instructions on the box for thawing.

1 sheet frozen puff
   pastry, thawed
1 small round of Brie
1/2 cup orange
   marmalade

1 slice candied
   citrus (optional)
1 egg

Preheat oven to 350°F. Prepare thawed pastry by unfolding it and cutting off one-third; set aside.

Cover the entire top of the cheese round in orange marmalade. Moving carefully and quickly, flip it over onto the waiting pastry sheet so the jammy top is now on the bottom. Take the pastry and fold all of the sides up and over the Brie, encasing the entire concoction. Now flip that entire thing over onto a baking sheet. If it is lined with parchment, all the better. Add a round piece of candied citrus to the top for an extra flourish, but it's not entirely necessary if you cannot find one. Almost there. Now crack and egg into a bowl and add a splash of water; beat together to make an egg wash. Brush the egg mixture over the top and sides of the pastry, as this will really help it to brown. Bake for 20 to 30 minutes, or until puffy and golden brown. Let sit for a bit before serving so the cheese is not too hot. It really is best warm, but room temperature is fine too.

CHOCOLATE CHIP–LADEN BANANA BREAD

3 ripe bananas
1 egg
1 cup sugar
4 tablespoons melted butter
2 teaspoons vanilla extract
1 1/2 cups all-purpose flour
1 teaspoon baking soda
1/16 to 1/8 teaspoon salt
1 (11- to 12-ounce) bag
   milk chocolate chips

Preheat oven to 325°F. Butter a loaf pan or round cake pan. (We did not have a loaf shaped pan, so I used a round cake pan. Use whatever you like.)

Mush up 3 ripe bananas in a good-size mixing bowl. To that, add 1 egg, 1 cup sugar, 4 tablespoons of melted butter (which is half a stick), and a good splash or two of vanilla extract. (We are Watkins fans, having sold it at the shop since we first opened.) Set aside.

In another bowl, put in 1 1/2 cups of all-purpose flour with 1 teaspoon baking soda and a big pinch of salt. Mix those three dry ingredients together. Now slowly mix the dry mixture into the banana mixture until fully incorporated. (I like to do this by hand, not using a mixer, to keep it as simple as possible.) Then mix in a bag of the best milk chocolate chips you can get your hands on. (I am a big fan of Ghirardelli brand.) Now it is ready to be put into the butter-greased pan. Bake for 45 minutes, or until a toothpick inserted in the center comes out clean. (Note: Cooking time will be shorter in a round cake pan.)

HALIBUT WITH LEMON & HERBS

MAKES 2 SERVINGS

Using fresh herbs in your cooking can be such a delight. The mellowness of using fresh herbs instead of dried can make all the difference in a dish. We plant more and more herbs in our zinc planter box. Some do not make it through the winter, while others do remarkably well, depending how cold it gets in Seattle area. We like thyme and oregano, among others, and the box overflows with herby goodness. Even having a few little pots of herbs in your kitchen, which you can pick up at your favorite garden nursery or grocer, can really elevate many dishes of summer. Try this super simple halibut dish day using some of your fresh herbs. You can substitute any white fish. The herbs infuse the meat of the fish, adding a nice earthiness and freshness.

2 halibut steaks
Salt
Extra-virgin olive oil
2 lemons

Sprigs fresh thyme
Sprigs fresh oregano
Jasmine or basmati rice, for serving

Preheat oven to 400 degrees. Lightly coat a baking dish with olive oil.

Place halibut steaks in a baking dish and sprinkle a healthy amount of salt over both sides of the fish. Let sit for a few minutes. Add a few glugs of extra-virgin olive oil to the top of the fish and the juice of half a lemon over each piece of halibut. Also thinly slice a lemon and remove the seeds from the slices. Set on top of halibut. Place sprigs of thyme and oregano around the fish. Done. It is that easy. Bake for 20 minutes, or a tad more or less depending on the thickness of your halibut steaks, until the fish is opaque. This is lovely served over jasmine or basmati rice. Enjoy those herbs!

"People who love to eat are always
the best people." –Julia Child

SHRIMP, PEAS & MINT RISOTTO

MAKES 4 TO 6 SERVINGS

1 pound (21 to 25 pieces) raw
  shrimp, peeled and deveined
Extra-virgin olive oil
Salt
Freshly ground black pepper
8 cups chicken stock
2 tablespoons butter

2 cups Arborio rice
1 cup white wine
1 (12-ounce) bag frozen peas
1 cup freshly grated Parmesan
  cheese, plus more for serving
Fresh mint, roughly
  chopped, for serving

Preheat the oven to 400°F.

Toss the shrimp in a bowl with extra-virgin olive oil and pinches of salt and pepper. Then spread shrimp on a baking sheet. Roast for about 6 minutes, until beginning to turn pink. Undercook them a bit, as they will continue to cook when you add them to the hot risotto toward the end. Set aside.

The same is true for the bag of frozen peas. They will cook from the heat of the rice. Here is my go-to recipe below.

In a medium saucepan, heat up the chicken stock to not quite boiling. Then turn down the heat a bit. Keep the stock hot through the entire risotto cooking process.

In a good-size cooking pot (I like to use a Le Creuset pot for cooking the risotto) over medium heat, melt the butter with $1/4$ cup extra-virgin olive oil. Add 2 cups Arborio rice to the pot and coat the rice with the butter-oil mixture. Sauté for 1 to 2 minutes to heat through, but don't brown the rice. All of the above is done over medium heat, but stove tops vary greatly, so adjust accordingly.

Now the liquids begin. Add 1 cup of white wine to the mixture. (I like to use a white that we will be serving with the meal.) Stir rice till the wine is absorbed. The depth of flavor the wine adds to the finished product is really noticeable.

The waiting hot stock now takes center stage. Add 1 cup of stock to the mixture, stirring till the stock is fully absorbed. What holds many folks back about making risotto is there is a good amount of stirring involved. A constant stir is not necessary, but pretty close. This is where the white wine you opened comes in quite nicely. Sipping a little during the risotto-making process is an enjoyable break from stirring. Continue adding the hot stock 1 cup at a time in this manner, and the rice will release its natural starches and become creamier as you go. When you add the sixth cup of stock, add the almost-cooked shrimp to the mixture. At this point, you will be about 20 to 25 minutes into the rice-cooking process. You are almost there.

Add the bag of peas. They do not need to be completely thawed, as the peas will defrost the moment they hit the hot rice. Stir. Add a cup of freshly grated Parmesan cheese. Stir. Turn off the heat. Add another cup of stock. Stir. Add a dusting of salt and freshly ground black pepper. Stir. Cover with the lid. Let sit for 5 minutes, have another sip of your white wine, as we are almost done. Once those 5 minutes have passed, give it one last stir, adding your last cup of stock so it is nice and creamy.

To serve, spoon risotto mixture into individual bowls. Add some of the largest shrimp to each bowl, and to finish, a few sprinkles of grated Parmesan along with a scattering of the fresh mint.

Here are some of our favorite risotto combinations:

Dungeness Crab Risotto

Risotto with Fresh Asparagus & Peas

Morel, Portobello & Saffron Risotto

Chive & Pea Risotto with Garlicky Shrimp

Leek & Asparagus Risotto

Butternut Squash & Sausage Risotto

Corn & Shrimp Risotto

WHERE TO SHOP

WATSON KENNEDY, of course! Peruse the website for thousands of goods. www.watsonkennedy.com

RESTAURANT SUPPLY STORES For votives and clear glass votive holders.

ANTIQUE STORES For vintage tabletop goods with history.

FLEA MARKETS A phenomenal way to fill a table and home with great vintage finds.

TAG SALES For incredible deals. Recycling at its finest.

ANTHROPOLOGIE Cool housewares abound. www.anthropologie.com

CB2 Glasses and plates galore. Great for stocking up for a party. www.cb2.com

CREEL AND GOW A bit like walking into a dream. Color and style abound. www.creelandgow.com

CURSIVE NEW YORK Whimsical and colorful goods great for gift-giving. www.cursivenewyork.com

DEMPSEY & CARROLL When you want the very best stationery. www.dempseyandcarroll.com

EBAY For when you know what you want and want to hunt it down. www.ebay.com

ETSY Creative, artisan-made goods at your fingertips. www.etsy.com

GLASSYBABY These iconic vessels will brighten any table they grace. www.glassybaby.com

HERMES If it is from here, it will be stupendous. www.hermes.com

HUDSON GRACE Fab shops & website for stylish tableware. www.hudsongracesf.com

JOHN DERIAN John's eye is amazing in all he does. His shops are a visual treat. www.johnderian.com

KRB Delightful art, furniture & objects. www.krbnyc.com

PAPER TRAIL A lovely assortment of just-right gifts to give. www.papertrailrhinebeck.com

POTTERY BARN They have been a go-to for staple goods for years. www.potterybarn.com

RED CHAIR ON WARREN I can't go to Hudson and not stop in. Absolute heaven. www.redchair-antiques.com

REED SMYTHE & COMPANY Artisan-made tabletop goods with tons of style. www.reedsmythe.com

SCULLY & SCULLY A NYC institution. The catalog is full of classic treats. www.scullyandscully.com

SUE FISHER KING A must-stop to shop when in San Francisco. www.suefisherking.com

SUR LA TABLE For utilitarian tabletop goods. www.surlatable.com

TORY BURCH Her tabletop goods are preppy and gorgeously made. www.toryburch.com

WILLIAMS SONOMA For all things tabletop, kitchen, and home. www.williams-sonoma.com

THE PROUST QUESTIONNAIRE

This is one of our favorite activities at the dining table when we are hosting a supper. We go around the table and ask questions to the guests from the Proust Questionnaire. We have a long list of questions so even the hosts get asked. It is a fun way to get to know folks better, even if they are your closest friends. Mister Google has tons of questions to add to the list. I'll start the party off!

YOUR IDEA OF HAPPINESS? Being surrounded by those I love, at the dining table, candles flickering, glasses full, flowers all about, and laughter filling the air.

YOUR FAVORITE COLOR? For those who know me well, they will not be surprised by this answer: Green tops the list. To me it signifies growth. There are so many glorious shades of the hue.

YOUR FAVORITE FLOWER? Major tie between tulips and peonies, with dahlias and hydrangeas right up at the top too.

WHERE WOULD YOU LIKE TO LIVE? In the city, in the country, and on the water.

YOUR IDEA OF MISERY? To be hungry. It is a problem in our world that we must solve.

WHAT DO YOU APPRECIATE MOST IN YOUR FRIENDS? Laughter and loyalty in the good and bad times.

YOUR FAVORITE PAINTERS? Matisse and Hugo Guinness. I feel very fortunate to call Hugo a friend; we have many of his works on our walls at home and at the shops.

YOUR FAVORITE PROSE AUTHORS? Ann Patchett, David Sedaris, Adam Gopnik.

YOUR FAVORITE OCCUPATION(S)? I am incredibly blessed that I get to do them. Shopkeeper, author, stylist, seeker of stylish goods.

WHAT OR WHO IS THE GREATEST LOVE OF YOUR LIFE? I feel lucky to have been married to him for 35 years now.

WHAT IS YOUR MOST TREASURED POSSESSION? The Rolex watch my parents gave to me on my twenty-first birthday. I have worn it every day since. It makes me think of them every time I put it on.

WHAT IS IT THAT YOU MOST DISLIKE? People who waste my time. I value time tremendously.

WHICH TALENT WOULD YOU MOST LIKE TO HAVE? I am laughing so hard as I type this. To sing. I have absolutely none of this talent.

WHAT IS YOUR MOST MARKED CHARACTERISTIC? Being optimistic.

IF YOU WERE TO DIE AND COME BACK AS A PERSON OR A THING, WHAT WOULD IT BE? A miniature Schnauzer with two dads.

WHO ARE YOUR HEROES IN REAL LIFE? Doctors and nurses, always. But even more so in the last few years.

WHICH LIVING PERSON DO YOU MOST ADMIRE? Those who work to make the world a better place for everyone.

WHAT IS YOUR MOTTO? Live in the moment.

SENDING MY LOVE & THANKS

If you bought or gave this book as a gift, a huge *thanks*. Books are truly a labor of love, and being able to share it with you means the world to me.

To all of you who have read the daily blog, follow along on social media, or are customers of WK—a big THANK YOU. I feel like we are on an adventure together. A really fun trip! It is a joy to have all of you along for the ride. Thank you for all the love and support you have shown me over the years in so many ways.

To the Watson Kennedy family, for keeping the ship going each and every day, but especially when I was away so much working on these pages. It takes a village, and I am honored to have the most amazing, talented, kind, hard-working, fun folks in mine. Abby, Barb, Brent, Carol Sue, Chelsea, Elizabeth, Erika, Gerrie, Heather, Lisa, Mimy, Olivia, Sarah, Shelby, Sophia, Sydney, Terence, Tim, Walter—I truly can't thank you each enough for all you do to keep things in tip-top shape.

To caretakers Steven, Bill, and Adrienne for keeping our homes extra spiffy, even when they look more like a photography studio at times.

To my friend Lisa Birnbach, who wrote such lovely, funny things. If you had told my teenage self that the author of *The Official Preppy Handbook* would write the foreword to one of my books, I would not have believed it. Thank you for your smart and witty worldview that always makes me laugh so hard. I adore you.

To Charlotte Moss and Margaret Russell, your words on the back of the book are beyond kind. You are each a powerhouse in the field of design, and I am so honored you took the time to write such thoughtful observations. *Merci, merci, merci*. I look forward to breaking bread with you both.

To my wonderful editor, Madge Baird, for all the support, direction, and expertise. You have been so respectful of my process all along the way. Ryan Thomann, art director extraordinaire, for getting inside my head and seeing what I saw for this book and for making it come to life. Chief Creative Officer Suzanne Gibbs Taylor at Gibbs Smith, major thanks for feeling the love and saying, "I want you to make books with us!" when we first met on that eventful day at the First & Spring shop. Indeed, we will. I feel like we have only just begun.

To our pooch, Bailey, who was at my side the entire time I was working on this book. Her devotion is just extraordinary.

And to Mister Sive, there is not enough room on this page to even begin my thanks. You have been my biggest cheerleader and partner in all of this since day one. You make my life sweeter each day, my love.

"There's only one thing more precious than our time and that's who we spend it with."
—Leo Christopher